SELF-LOVE JOURNAL

WHY YOU ARE SO DAMN WORTHY

How to Adopt Positive Thinking, Gain Self-Esteem, and Self-Confidence In Adversity

JAN FOSTER

Copyright © 2020 Jan Foster

All Rights Reserved

Copyright 2020 By Jan Foster - All rights reserved.

The following book is produced below with the goal of providing information that is as accurate and reliable as possible. Regardless, purchasing this eBook can be seen as consent to the fact that both the publisher and the author of this book are in no way experts on the topics discussed within and that any recommendations or suggestions that are made herein are for entertainment purposes only. Professionals should be consulted as needed prior to undertaking any of the action endorsed herein.

This declaration is deemed fair and valid by both the American Bar Association and the Committee of Publishers Association and is legally binding throughout the United States.

Furthermore, the transmission, duplication or reproduction of any of the following work including specific information will be considered an illegal act irrespective of if it is done electronically or in print. This extends to creating a secondary or tertiary copy of the work or a recorded copy and is only allowed with express written consent from the Publisher. All additional right reserved.

The information in the following pages is broadly considered to be a truthful and accurate account of facts and as such any inattention, use or misuse of the information in question by the reader will render any resulting actions solely under their purview. There are no scenarios in which the publisher or the original author of this work can be in any fashion deemed liable for any hardship or damages that may befall them after undertaking information described herein.

Additionally, the information in the following pages is intended only for informational purposes and should thus be thought of as universal. As befitting its nature, it is presented without assurance regarding its prolonged validity or interim quality. Trademarks that are mentioned are done without written consent and can in no way be considered an endorsement from the trademark holder.

Table of Contents

PART I 13

Chapter 1: Self-Care Is the Best Care 14

    How Does Self-Care Work 15

    How Does Self-Care Improve Self-Esteem and Self-Confidence? 16

Chapter 2: 19

What Does Good Self-Care Look Like? 19

    Good Self-Care Practices 19

        Taking Responsibility for Your Happiness 19

        You Become Assertive With Others 19

        You Treat Yourself As You Would a Close Friend 19

        You Are Not Afraid to Ask for What You Want 20

        Your Life Is Set Around Your Own Values 20

Chapter 3: Demanding Your Own Self-Care 21

    Setting Healthy Boundaries 21

        Identify and Name Your Limits 21

        Stay Tuned Into Your Feelings 22

        Don't Be Afraid of Being Direct 22

        Give Yourself Permission to Set Boundaries 22

        Consider Your Past and Present 23

        Be Assertive 23

        Start Small 23

    Eliminating Toxicity and Not Caring About Losing Friends 24

        Don't Expect People to Change 24

Establish and Maintain Boundaries 24

Don't Keep Falling for Crisis Situations 24

Focus on the Solution 25

Accept Your Own Difficulties and Weaknesses 25

They Won't Go Easily 25

Choose Your Battles Carefully 26

Surround Yourself With Healthy relationships 26

How to Focus on Self-Care 26

Pay Attention to Your Sleep 26

Take Care of Your Gut 27

Exercise and Physical Activity Is Essential 27

Consider a Mediterranean Diet 27

Take a Self-Care Trip 28

Get Outside 28

Bring a Pet Into Your Life 28

Get Yourself Organized 28

Cook Yourself Meals At Home 28

Read Regularly 29

Schedule Your Self-Care Time 29

Chapter 4: How to Be Happy Being Alone 30

Accept Some Alone Time 30

Do Not Compare Yourself to Others 30

Step Away From Social Media 30

Take a Break From Your Phone 31

Allow Time for Your Mind to Wander 31

Take Yourself on a Date 31

Exercise 31

Take Advantage of the Perks of Being Alone 31

Find a Creative Outlet 32

Take Time to Self-Reflect 32

Make Plans for Your Future 32

Make Plans for Solo Outings 32

PART II 35

Chapter 1: Energy Healing- The Key to Holistic Health 36

Chapter 2: Energy Healing and Overcoming Suffering 38

Energy and Grief/Trauma 38

Energy and Mental Health 39

Daily Energy Regulation 40

Chapter 3: The Daily Energy Healing Journey 42

Understanding Your Energy Field: Daily Energy Healing Meditation with Journaling (Week 5) 42

Protecting Your Energy Field: Daily Energy Healing Meditation with Journaling (Week 6) 44

Healing Through Trapped Emotion Release: Daily Energy Healing Meditation with Journaling (Week 7) 45

Cultivating Self-Trust in your Healing Journey: Daily Energy Healing Meditation With Journaling (Week 8) 47

Mini Meditation Toolbox: 25 Quick and Easy Energy Restoration and Protection Meditations 49

Chapter 1- What is Self Compassion 67

The Three Elements of Self-Compassion 68

Discovering Self Compassion 69

Conclusion 70

Chapter 2- Benefits of Self-Compassion 71

Self-Compassion At Work 72

    Self-Compassion In Relationships...73

    Self-Compassion In Life..74

Chapter 3: Myths about Self Compassion 76

    #1 Self-Compassion is just a person crying out for self-pity 76

    #2 Self-compassion is a sign of weakness..77

    #3 Self-Compassion can make you a complacent person....................78

    #5 Self-compassion makes us selfish..80

    Conclusion..82

Chapter 4- Dealing with Negativity..83

    What Can Negative Thinking do to your Brain? 83

    What Can Positive Thinking do to your Brain?.....................................84

    Steps to deal with Negative thoughts and Events................................86

    Learn to Forgive Yourself..88

    Steps to Overcome Failure...90

    Surrounding yourself with Positive People...92

    Your GOOD Category 92

    Think About How You Interact with People...93

    Benefits of surrounding yourself with Positive People 94

Chapter 5: Building and Mastering Emotions 96

    The Five Categories of Emotional Intelligence (EQ) 96

    Self-regulation includes: 97

    Motivation is made up of:...97

    Creating a Balance with Emotional Awareness....................................99

    Conclusion...102

Chapter 6: Practical steps for Becoming self compassionate................. 103

    Practicing Creative Visualization to Encourage Self-Compassion 107

    Concise Guidelines for Creative Visualization:...................................110

- Using Affirmations ... 111
- Making Affirmations Work for You ... 113
- Examples of Positive Affirmation ... 114
- Mindfulness Meditation for Self-Compassion ... 115
- Exercise 1 – Mindful Breathing ... 115
- Exercise 2 – Awareness ... 116
- Exercise 3 – Mental Focus ... 118

Chapter 1: Self-Esteem and Valuing Yourself ... 121

- How Low Self-Esteem Is Developed ... 123
  - The Different Types of Parents ... 123
  - Bullying ... 124
  - Trauma ... 126
  - The Science of Self-Esteem ... 128

Chapter 2: How You Can Matter to Yourself ... 130

- How to Build Self-Awareness ... 131
  - Recognize What Bothers You About Other People ... 131
  - Meditate on Your Mind ... 132
  - Draw a Timeline of Your Life ... 133
  - Identify Your Emotional Kryptonite ... 133
  - Travel and Get Out a Little Bit ... 134
  - Pick Up a New Skill ... 134
  - Clarify Your True Values ... 134

Chapter 3: Creating a Stronger Self ... 136

- Managing Your Ego ... 136
  - Don't Take Things Personally ... 137
  - Accepts All of Your Mistakes ... 137
  - Stop Being Self-Conscious ... 137

- Realize That Your Ego Will Never Go Away 139
- You Are Not the Best 139
- Imagine Your Ego as Another Person 139
- Stop Bragging 140
- Be Grateful for the Little Things 140
- Learn to Compliment Others 140
- Forgiving People 141
- Overcoming Trauma 144

Chapter 4: Changing Our Minds 147

- How To Ignore Things 147
  - Stop Comparing Yourself To Others 147
  - Ignore Societal Pressure 148
  - Start Living In The Present Moment 149
  - Leverage Your Purpose 149
- The Mindset Shift 150
- Now That Your Self-Esteem is High 151

Chapter 1: Why So Sensitive? 155

- How To Tell If You're In The Camp 156
- What Makes People Overly Sensitive? 158
- Negative Aspects Of Being A Highly Sensitive Person 160
  - In The Workplace 160
  - In Their Personal Lives 162

Chapter 2: Embrace Your Sensitivities 164

- Benefits Of Being a Highly Sensitive Person 164
  - Having A Depth Of Experience And Feelings 165
  - Self-Awareness 165

- Intuitive Nurturing Skills 165
- A Knack For Forming Close relationships 165
- Appreciating The Small Things In Life 166
- Why Highly Sensitive People Make Great Friends 166
- Why Highly Sensitive People Make Great Employees 167

Chapter 3: Living As A Highly Sensitive Person 169

- How To Overcome Your Sensitivities 169
- Having Self-Esteem As A Highly Sensitive Person 171
  - Accept Thoughts, Emotions, And Sensations As They Are 172
  - Eliminate The Word "Should" From Your Vocabulary 172
  - Do Not Rely On Other People For Self-Esteem 172
  - Forgive 172
  - Take Stock Of Your Talents 173
- Focusing On Jobs, You Are Good At 173
  - Caring Professions 174
  - Creative Endeavors 174
  - Clergy 174
  - Academia 174
  - IT Professional 175
- Dealing With Hyperarousal 175
  - Practice Mindfulness 176
  - Make Small Achievable Goals Towards Relaxation And Calmness 177
  - Positive Self-Talk 177
  - Investigate The Root Cause 178

PART I

Chapter 1: Self-Care Is the Best Care

"It is so important to take time for yourself and find clarity. The most important relationship is the one you have with yourself."

-Diane Von Furstenberg

Self-care is any activity that we deliberately do to improve our own well-being, whether it is physical, emotional, mental, or spiritual. The importance of taking care of one's self cannot be denied, as even health care training focuses on making sure healthcare workers are caring for themselves. If you do not take care of yourself, eventually, every other aspect o your life will fall apart, including your ability to help others.

This is a very simple concept, yet it is highly overlooked in the grand scheme of things. People lack the tendency to look after themselves and put their needs before anyone else. Good self-care is essential to improving our mood and reducing our anxiety levels. It will do wonders for reducing exhaustion and burnout, which is very common in our fast-paced world. It will also lead to positive improvements in our relationships.

One thing to note is that self-care does not mean forcing ourselves to do something we don't like, no matter how enjoyable it is to other people. For example, if your friends are forcing you to go to a party you rather not attend, then giving in is not taking care of yourself. If you would rather stay in and watch a movie, then that's what you should do, and it will be better for your well-being.

How Does Self-Care Work

It is difficult to pinpoint exactly what self-care is, as it is personal for everybody. Some people love to pamper themselves by going to the spa, while others enjoy physical activities like hiking, biking, or swimming. Some individuals take up art or other hobbies, like writing or playing a musical instrument. These activities are all different but will have the same type of benefits for the individuals engaging in them.

The main factor to consider when engaging in self-care is to determine if you enjoy the activity in question. If not, then it's time to move on. Self-care is an active choice that you actually have to plan out. It is time you set aside for yourself to make sure all of your needs are met. If you use a planner of any sort, make sure to dedicate some space for your particular self-care activities. Also, let people who need to know about your plans so you can become more committed. Pay special attention to how you feel afterward. The objective of any self-care activity is to make yourself feel better. If this is not happening, then it's time to change the activity.

While self-care, as a whole, is individualized, there is a basic checklist to consider.

- Create a list of things you absolutely don't want to do during the self-care process. For instance, not checking emails, not answering the phone, avoiding activities you don't enjoy, or not going to specific gatherings, like a house party.
- Eat nutritious and healthy meals most of the time, while indulging once in a while.
- Get the proper amount of sleep according to your needs.
- Avoid too many negative things, like news or social media.
- Exercise regularly.
- Spend appropriate time with your loved ones. These are the people you genuinely enjoy and not forced relationships.
- Look for opportunities to enjoy yourself and laugh.
- Do at least one relaxing activity a day, like taking a bath, going for a walk, or cooking a meal.

Self-care is extremely important and should not be an anomaly in your life.

How Does Self-Care Improve Self-Esteem and Self-Confidence?

To bring everything full circle, self-care plays a major role in improving self-esteem and self-confidence. It is easy to see how taking care of yourself will also make you feel better about yourself overall. All of these are actually inter-related, and a lack of one showcases a lack of the other. While caring for yourself also improves your self-esteem and self-confidence, not having self-esteem or self-confidence also leads to a lack of self-care. Basically, you believe that you are not good enough to be taken care of.

People with high self-esteem and self-confidence value themselves as much as they value others, and have no issues with making sure they're taken care of. They realize that it does not make them selfish or inconsiderate to think in this manner. Even if other people try to make them feel that way, a self-confident person will just brush off the criticism. An important thing to note is that when you take care of yourself, it does not mean you don't care about other people. It simply means you have enough self-love to not place yourself on the backburner.

Many people work so hard to try and please everyone else. This is one of the telltale signs of low self-esteem. While they're busy worried about other peoples' needs, their own get neglected, which will wear them down over time. The more they're unable to please someone, the harder they will try. What people in this situation don't realize is that some people are impossible to please, and it is not their responsibility to please them. That is up to the individual.

Poor self-care will eventually lead to poor self-image. It is possible that a person already has this initially. Self-care includes taking care of your hygienic and grooming needs. If you don't take the time to make yourself look good, this will significantly impact the value you place on yourself. When you are t work, among your friends, or just walking around town, not feeling like you look good will ultimately make you feel like you don't belong anywhere. Your confidence levels will plummet due to this.

Your health is another aspect to consider. Poor self-care means bad sleeping habits, unhealthy diets, lack of exercise, and more self-destructive behaviors. Your poor health practices can result in chronic illnesses down the line, like heart disease or diabetes. Once again, diminished health will lead to reduced self-confidence and self-esteem. Ask yourself now if putting other people ahead of you is worth it? I've got some news for you. The people who demand the most from you are probably looking out for themselves first.

The less a person takes care of themselves, the more their self-esteem and self-confidence will decline. It turns into a vicious downward cycle. This is why it is important to focus on all of these areas equally. When you find yourself neglecting your own self-care practices, it is time to shift your direction and bring your attention back to your needs. Ignoring your needs will ultimately lead to your fall. We will discuss specific practices and techniques for improving self-care in the next chapter.

Chapter 2:

What Does Good Self-Care Look Like?

Good Self-Care Practices

The following are some ways that good self-care will look like. If you find yourself having these qualities, then you are on the right path.

Taking Responsibility for Your Happiness

When you engage in self-care, it is truly self-care. This means you only rely on yourself, and nobody else, to make sure your needs are met. You realize that your happiness is no one else's responsibility but your own. You alone have the ability to control your outcomes. As a result of this independence, you will develop the skills and attitude you need to care for your own physical, mental, emotional, and spiritual well-being.

You Become Assertive With Others

People often take assertiveness for rudeness. This is not true, but if people believe that standing firm for what you want is rude, then that's their problem. Once you reach a certain mindset where self-care is important to you, then you will be unapologetically assertive. This means you have the ability to say "no" with confidence and stand by it. "No" is a complete sentence, and people will realize that quickly when they hear it from you.

You Treat Yourself As You Would a Close Friend

It's interesting how we believe that other people deserve better treatment from us than we do ourselves. We have a tendency to put our best friends in front of us, no matter how detrimental it is to our lives. This behavior stops once we engage in proper self-care. At this point, you will treat yourself as good as, or even better, than you treat your most beloved friends.

You Are Not Afraid to Ask for What You Want

Once you learn to take care of yourself, you also see your value increase within your mind. This means having an understanding that your voice, opinion, and needs matter, just like anybody with high self-esteem and self-confidence, would. As a result, you will not be afraid to ask for what you want, even if you might not get it.

Your Life Is Set Around Your Own Values

Once you practice self-care, you learn to check in with yourself before making important decisions. You always make sure the choices you are about to make line up with your purpose and values. If they go against them, then it's not a path you choose. This goes for the career you choose, where you decide to live, and the relationships you maintain in your life.

While all of the traits are focused on self, but it will lead to better relationships with other people too. When you practice self-care, you are in a better state in every aspect of your being. This gives you the ability to take care of and help those you need you, as well. Self-care is not an option, but a necessity, and it must never be ignored. Taking care of yourself is not selfish, no matter what anybody tells you. If someone tries to make you feel guilty over this matter, then consider distancing or removing them from your life. You are not obligated to maintain relationships with people.

Chapter 3: Demanding Your Own Self-Care

We went over the importance of self-care, and now we will focus on making it a reality in your life. If you want self-care to occur, you must be willing to demand it. The world is full of people who expect you to be at there beck-and-call every moment of the day. Some of these individuals are those who are closest to us, like friends or family members. This can make it harder to make our demands heard, but there is no way around it. Taking care of yourself is not an idea you can budge on. It is extremely important. We will go over several ways to maintain your ability for self-care in your life and provide detailed action steps to help you progress in this area.

Setting Healthy Boundaries

One of the biggest obstacles to self-care is other people who surround you. These are the true selfish individuals, whether they realize it or not, who believe they can barge in on your life and deserve all of your attention. They will take advantage of you, and if you are not careful, they will completely gain control of your emotions, and even your life. For proper self-care to occur, you must set firm and healthy boundaries with people. The following are steps that need to become mainstays in your life.

Identify and Name Your Limits

You must understand what your emotional, physical, mental, and spiritual limits are. If you do not know, then you will never be able to set real boundaries with people. Determine what behaviors you can tolerate and accept, and then consider what makes you feel uncomfortable. Identifying and separating these traits will help us determine our lines.

Stay Tuned Into Your Feelings

Two major emotions that are red flags that indicate a person is crossing a barrier are resentment or discomfort. Whenever you are having these feelings, it is important to determine why. Resentment generally comes from people taking advantage of us or feelings of being unappreciated. In this instance, we are likely pushing ourselves beyond our limits because we feel guilty. Guilt-trips is a weapon that many people use to get their way. It is important to recognize when someone is trying to make you feel guilty because they are way overstepping their boundaries. Resentment could also be due to someone imposing their own views or values onto us. When someone makes you feel uncomfortable, that is another indication of a boundary crossed. Stay in tune with both of these emotions.

Don't Be Afraid of Being Direct

With some people, setting boundaries is easy because they have a similar communication style. They can simply read your cues and back off when needed. For other individuals, a more direct approach is needed. Some people just don't get the hint that they've crossed a line. You must communicate to them in a firm way that they have crossed your limits, and you need some space. A respectful person will honor your wishes without hesitation. If they don't, then that's on them. Your personal space is more important than their feelings.

Give Yourself Permission to Set Boundaries

The potential downfalls to personal limits are fear, self-doubt, and guilt. We may fear the other person's response when we set strong boundaries. Also, we may feel guilty if they become emotional about it. We may even have self-doubt on whether we can maintain these limits in the long run. Many individuals have the mindset that in order to be a good daughter, son, parent, or friend, etc., we have to say "yes" all the time. They often wonder if they deserve to have boundaries and limits with those closest to them. The answer is, yes, you do. You need to give yourself permission to set limits with people because they are essential to maintaining healthy relationships too. Boundaries are also a sign of self-respect. Never feel bad for respecting yourself.

Consider Your Past and Present

Determine what roles you have played throughout your life in the various relationships you have had. Were you the one who was always the caretaker? If so, then your natural tendency may be to put others before yourself. Also, think about your relationships now. Are you the one always taking care of things, or is it a reciprocal relationship? For example, are you always the one making plans, buying gifts, having dinner parties, and being responsible for all of the important aspects of the relationships? If this is the case, then tuning into your needs is especially important here. If you are okay with the dynamics of the relationship, then that's fine. I can't tell you how to feel. However, if you feel anger and resentment over this, then it's time to let your feeling be known, unapologetically.

Be Assertive

Once again, this does not mean being rude, even though some people will interpret it that way. Being assertive simply means being firm, which is important when reminding someone about your boundaries. Creating boundaries alone is not enough. You also have to stand by them and let people know immediately if they've crossed them. Let the person know in a respectful but strong tone that you are uncomfortable with where they're going, and they need to give you some space. Assertive communication is a necessity.

Start Small

Setting boundaries is a skill that takes a while to develop, especially if it's something you've never done before. Therefore, start with a small boundary, like no phone calls after a certain time at night. Make sure to follow through;

otherwise, the boundary is worthless. From here, make larger boundaries based on your comfort level.

Eliminating Toxicity and Not Caring About Losing Friends

If you plan on making self-care a priority in your life, I think that's great, and so should you. However, some people will have a problem with this. People don't always like it when their friends, family members, or acquaintances, etc., put themselves at the forefront of their lives. Once again, that is their problem, not yours. What is your problem, though, is distancing or even eliminating these individuals from your life. We will go over that in this section because part of self-care is eliminating toxicity from your life and not feeling bad about it.

Don't Expect People to Change

While everyone deserves a chance to redeem themselves, there comes the point where we must accept that people cannot change by force. They have to find it within themselves to make this change, and it is not our responsibility to do so. You may yearn to be the one who changes them, but it's usually a hopeless project. Toxic individuals are motivated by their problems. They use them to get the attention they need. Stop being the one to give it to them.

Establish and Maintain Boundaries

I already went in-depth on this, so I won't revisit it too much here. Just know that toxic people will push you to work harder and harder for them, while you completely ignore your own needs. This is exhausting and unacceptable. Create the boundaries you need with these individuals based on your own limits.

Don't Keep Falling for Crisis Situations

Toxic people will make you feel like they need you always because they are constantly in a crisis situation of some sort. It is a neverending cycle. When a person is in a perpetual crisis, it is of their own doing. They often create drama purposely to get extra attention. You may feel guilty for ignoring them, but remember that their being manipulative and not totally genuine.

I am not saying that you can't ever help someone who is going through a hard time. Of course, you can. Just don't start believing that you're responsible for their success or failure.

Focus on the Solution

Toxic individuals will give you a lot to be angry and sad about. If you focus on this, then you will just become miserable. You must focus on the solution, which, in this case, is removing drama and toxicity from your life. Recognize the fact that you will have less emotional stress once you remove this person from your life. If you let them, they will suck away all of your energy.

Accept Your Own Difficulties and Weaknesses

A toxic person will know how to exploit your weaknesses and use them against you. For example, if you are easy to guilt-trip, they will have you feel guilty every time you pull away from them. If you get to know yourself better and recognize these weaknesses, then you can better manage them and protect yourself. This goes along with creating self-awareness, which we discussed in chapter two. When you accept your weaknesses, you can work on fixing them and balance them with your strengths.

They Won't Go Easily

Recognize that a toxic individual may resist being removed from your life. Actually, if they don't resist, I will be pleasantly surprised. They may throw tantrums, but this is because they can't control or manipulate you anymore. They will even increase their previous tactics with more intensity. It is a trap, and you must not fall for it. Stay firm in your desire to leave and keep pushing forward. If they suck you back in, good luck trying to get out again.

Choose Your Battles Carefully

Fighting with a toxic person is exhausting and usually not worth it. You do not need to engage in every battle with them. They are just trying to instigate you.

Surround Yourself With Healthy relationships

Once you have removed a toxic person, or persons, from your life, then avoid falling into the trap with someone else. Fill your circle with happy and healthy relationships, so there is no room for any toxicity. Always remember the signs of a toxic person, so you can avoid them wholeheartedly in the future.

How to Focus on Self-Care

Now that we have worked to set boundaries and eliminate toxic people from our lives, it is time to focus on ourselves and the self-care we provide. The following are some self-care tips, according to psychologist, Dr. Tchiki Davis, Ph.D.

Pay Attention to Your Sleep

Sleep is an essential part of taking care of yourself. You must make it part of your routine because it will play a huge role in your emotional and physical well-being. There are many things that can wreak havoc on your sleep patterns, like stress, poor diet, watching television, or looking at your phone as you're trying to fall asleep. Think about your night routine. Are you eating right before bed or taking in a lot of sugar and caffeine? Are you working nonstop right up until bedtime? Have you given yourself some time to wind down before going to sleep? All of these factors are important to consider, as they will affect your sleep patterns. If you can, put away any phones, tablets, and turn off the television at least 30 minutes before you plan on going to bed.

Take Care of Your Gut

We often neglect our digestive tract, but it plays a major role in our health and overall well-being. When our gut is not working well, it makes us feel sluggish, bloated, and nonproductive. Pay attention to the food you eat as it will determine the health of your gut. It is best to avoid food with excess salt, sugar, cholesterol, or unhealthy fats. Stick to foods that are high in fiber, protein, healthy fats, and complex carbs. Some good options are whole grains, nuts, lean meats, fruits and vegetables, beans, and fish.

Exercise and Physical Activity Is Essential

Regular exercise is great for both physical and mental health. The physical benefits are obvious. However, many people do not realize that exercise will help the body release certain hormones like endorphins and serotonin. These are often called feel-good hormones because they play a major role in affecting our mood in a positive way. The release of these hormones will give us energy too, which will make us want to exercise more. Once exercise becomes a habit, it will be hard to break. Decide for yourself what your exercise routine will be, whether it's going to the gym, walking around the neighborhood, or playing a game of tennis.

Consider a Mediterranean Diet

While this is not a dietary book, the Mediterranean diet is considered the healthiest diet in the world because of its extreme health benefits. The food groups and ingredients that are used will increase energy, brain function, and has amazing benefits like heart and digestive tract health. The food also does not lack flavor, which shatters the myth that healthy food does not taste good.

Take a Self-Care Trip

Even if you are not much of a traveler, getting away once in a while can do wonders for your mental health. So often, our environment will make us feel stressed out, and it's good to remove ourselves from it for a couple of days. You do not have to take a trip abroad here. Of course, that is certainly an option. A simple weekend trip is perfectly fine. Just get yourself out of your normal routine and be by yourself for a while.

Get Outside

Nature and sunlight can be great medicines. It can help you reduce stress or worry, and has many great health benefits. Doing some physical activity outside, like hiking or gardening, are also great options.

Bring a Pet Into Your Life

Pets can bring you a lot of joy, and the responsibility they come with can boost your self-confidence by having to care for another living creature. Dogs are especially great at helping to reduce stress and anxiety. Animal therapy has been used to help people suffering from disorders lie PTSD, as well.

Get Yourself Organized

Organizing your life and doing some decluttering can do wonders for your mental and emotional health. Decide what area of your life needs to be organized. Do you need to clear your desk, clean out the fridge, or declutter your closet? Do you need to get a calendar or planner and schedule your life better? Whatever you can do to get yourself more organized, do it. Being organized allows you to know how to take better care of yourself.

Cook Yourself Meals At Home

People often neglect the benefits of a good home-cooked meal. They opt, instead, for fast-food or microwave dinners. These types of meals will make you full but will lack in essential nutrients that your body needs. Cooking nutritious meals at home will allow you to use the correct ingredients, so you can feel full and satisfied. Cooking alone can also be great therapy for people.

Read Regularly

Self-help books are a great read. However, do not limit yourself to these. You can also read books on subjects that you find fascinating or books that simply provide entertainment.

Schedule Your Self-Care Time

Just like you would write down an appointment time in your planner, also block out specific times for self-care activities. Stick to this schedule religiously, unless a true emergency comes up. This means that if a friend calls you to go out, you should respectfully decline their request and focus on yourself.

Chapter 4: How to Be Happy Being Alone

The final section of this book will focus on being alone and how to be happy about it. When you start engaging in self-care, you will also be spending much more time by yourself. A lot of people have a hard time dealing with this concept, especially if they're used to being around people all the time. However, for proper self-care, you have to be okay with being alone once in a while.

Accept Some Alone Time

The following are some tips to help you become happy with being alone. Soon, you will realize that your own company is the best kind.

Do Not Compare Yourself to Others

We are referring to your social life here. Do not compare to others, and do not feel like you must live as others do. If you do this, you may become jealous of a person's social circle or lifestyle. It is better to focus on yourself and what makes you happy. If you plan on spending significant time alone, then you cannot pay attention to what other people are doing.

Step Away From Social Media

If strolling through your social media page makes you feel left out, then take a step back and put it away for a while. During self-care moments, you are the focus, not what is happening with others online. Also, what people post on their pages is not always true. Many individuals have been known to exaggerate, or even flat-out lie on social media platforms. You may be feeling jealous or left out for no reason. Try banning yourself from social media for 24-48 hours, and see how it makes you feel.

Take a Break From Your Phone

Avoid making or receiving calls. Let the important people in your life know that you will be away from your phone for a while, so they don't worry. When you are alone, really try to be alone.

Allow Time for Your Mind to Wander

If you feel unusual about doing nothing, it is probably because you have not allowed yourself to be in this position for a while. Carve out a small amount of time where you stay away from TV, music, the internet, and even books. Use this time to just sit quietly with your thoughts. Find a comfortable spot to sit or lie down, then just let your mind wander and see where it takes you. This may seem strange the first time, but with practice, you will get used to the new freedom.

Take Yourself on a Date

You don't need to be with someone else to enjoy a night out on the town. Take a self-date and enjoy your own company for a while. Go to a movie by yourself, stop by a nice restaurant, or just go do an activity you enjoy. If you are not used to hanging out alone, give it some time and you will become more comfortable with it. Take yourself on that solo date.

Exercise

We have mentioned exercise and physical activity a lot, but that's because it has so many great benefits related to self-care. Exercising will uplift your mood, and make it more enjoyable to be by yourself. Those feel-good hormones will provide a lot of benefits during these times.

Take Advantage of the Perks of Being Alone

Some people have spent so much time with other people that they've forgotten the perks of being alone. There are many to consider. First of all, you do not have to ask anyone's permission to do anything; you will have more personal space, can enjoy the activities you want to do, and don't have to worry about upsetting anyone. If you want, you can even have a solo dance party in your living room, Tom Cruise style. There are many advantages to being alone, so use them.

Find a Creative Outlet

It is beneficial to use some of your alone time to work on something creative. This can be painting, sculpting, music, writing, or any other creative endeavors. In fact, you can get out the watercolors and start fingerpainting. Creativity will bring a lot of joy into your life. It will make you happier about being alone.

Take Time to Self-Reflect

Being alone will give you the opportunity to self-reflect on your life. You won't care so much about being alone when you are coming up with important answers to your life.

Make Plans for Your Future

Planning out your life for five or ten years down the line will give you something important to do, and something to look forward to. Alone time is the perfect opportunity to determine these plans.

Make Plans for Solo Outings

Plan your solo outings based on what you like to do, whether it's a farmer's market, hiking, riding your bike, or going camping alone. Mak plans that will excite you, and you will be taking care of yourself while also being okay alone.

There are numerous topics that we went over in this chapter, but they all relate back to one theme: Self-care. Always remember that to take proper care of yourself, you must consider the following ideas:

- Setting Boundaries
- Avoiding and ridding yourself of toxic people
- Focus on yourself and your needs
- Be okay with being alone

Focus on these areas, and you will be demanding your own self-care without ever apologizing for it.

PART II

Chapter 1: Energy Healing- The Key to Holistic Health

Understanding the impacts of energy imbalances and corresponding physical, mental, spiritual health

How many times have you, or another adult in your life, said the words "I just don't have the energy I used to have."? Most adults know the feeling of looking at the energy children have as they run about, enjoying life, exploring their surroundings, and never seeming to grow tired. Many of us are left reflecting back on the distant past when we, too, had such energy and wondering where it went.

From the time children enter school, they begin to be presented with expectations. Stand in a straight line, raise your hand, don't talk while the teacher is talking. Each year, the level of responsibility and expectation seems to increase. While rules, regulations, and individual responsibility are important for a functioning society, there are numerous expectations and social pressures put on people as they grow, which can be incredibly harmful.

It is generally around middle school when children become more acutely aware of their bodies and societal beauty standards, which tell them what they "should" look like. Children are likely to become aware of the trends, such as which clothes the "cool kids" are wearing. The endless battle to feel like enough begins, and can lead to a plethora of issues with self-esteem, eating disorders, and mental illness. In addition to the basic societal pressures to be accepted and considered attractive, many children are also faced with difficult situations at home where their own needs are not being met, they are having to provide for and protect themselves in the only ways they know how, avoid abusive parents, care for younger siblings, or worry about if they'll have anything to eat that day. Even if children have a relatively healthy home life, this is the age when they will begin to become aware of the issues that plague their family (every family has issues) whether this is divorce, an alcoholic parent, the death of a pet or loved one, etc.

We live in a society that thrives off of consumerism. We are flooded with images of how the next vacation, new pair of shoes, nicer car, nicer house, or perfect partner will make us happy, and all of the things we need to change about ourselves in order to fulfill those things. Eventually, all the energy we had as a child starts going towards maintaining our image in society, trying to have all the "best" life has to offer (which always happens to be everything we do not have), and attempting to be as "successful" as possible in the eyes of society and other people. With no time to rest in the present moment, recharge, and appreciate what we already have, it is no wonder, so many of us are completely drained of energy. In such a fast-paced society that discourages breaks, our energy will become depleted, and we will find ourselves thrown out of balance and unable to obtain true happiness and well-being. Over time, this depletion and imbalance can lead to a sense of spiritual disconnection, extreme mental health issues, and an increased risk of physical pain, illness, and even earlier death.

Chapter 2: Energy Healing and Overcoming Suffering

Energy and Grief/Trauma

Every human being knows that loss is a natural part of life. The one certain thing in life is that we, and everyone we know, is going to die. However, in such a fast-paced society, we are often given a very short grace period before being expected to swallow our grief and "move on" when we lose those closest to us. It is not abnormal for people to receive a bereavement period of only a few days before being expected to be back in the classroom or office and be fully functional. There is very little space for the grief journey, and most people are expected to harbor their feelings and keep their grief to themselves.

The grief process is expansive and incredibly energy draining. When we don't receive the adequate support from those around us, or adequate space to heal, our body begins to break down piece by piece. The empty spaces within us will swallow us up into states of depression, numbness, isolation, and pure exhaustion. Just like a wound being denied the correct treatment and care, the wounds of unresolved grief will fester and leave us feeling completely drained of energy and vitality for life.

Unresolved trauma also has an incredibly destructive impact on the body. Trauma can occur as a result of grief itself, as well as emotional or domestic abuse, accident or illness, war, sexual assault, childhood maltreatment, etc. The body holds trauma in various places, and the brain switches over from the logical ability to discern safety and danger into an easily triggered emotional state. An overactive emotional brain loses the ability to think clearly, make decisions, and recognize threats. People who have unresolved trauma are likely to be easily triggered and deal with unexplained outbursts of anger, fear, relationship issues, reckless behavior, and health problems. When trauma sits in the body unresolved, the brain is unable to understand that the traumatic event has ended. Therefore, it will stay in a consistent fight-or-flight state, which is incredibly draining and will leave the body with no energy. Not only will trauma victims experience low energy levels, but they will also experience severe issues maintaining positive relationships and overall well-being.

Energy and Mental Health

There are numerous factors that can contribute to mental health issues. As previously discussed, societal issues and unresolved grief and trauma can yield higher levels of anxiety, depression, and PTSD. It is also very common for people to suffer from mood disorders, personality disorders, disordered eating, substance abuse, etc. The list is long for psychological ailments and how they happen, and it has been proven that 1 in 3 people will be diagnosed with a mental illness in their lifetime. Even without a specific disorder, most people will have periods of life where their mental health suffers greatly.

No matter what a person's struggle with mental health looks like, or what they are doing (or not doing) in terms of treatment, the body expends a lot of energy when a part of it is unwell.

Daily Energy Regulation

No matter what it is in your life that is causing you to feel depleted, it is vital to pay attention to the energy fields within the body and identify the areas of greatest pain and imbalance. In the spectrum of health, people often take measures such as going to see the doctor, therapist, or grief counselor, taking medication, and making lifestyle changes such as finding a hobby or increasing exercise. However, a piece that is commonly overlooked in the healing journey is healing energetically. No matter how much you invest in your mental, physical, emotional, and spiritual health, if your energies remain imbalanced, it is impossible to reach a state of full wellness. That being said, energy healing is the missing piece in most people's quests for holistic health.

In many cases, it can be beneficial to seek the help of energy healers, massage therapists, and reiki, craniosacral therapy, or bodywork practitioners. These practitioners are trained in getting in touch with your energy centers and helping bring them back into balance through healing touch, body movements, and visualization techniques. If you are dealing with energy imbalance, seeing a practitioner can be an excellent investment in unlocking your highest levels of health and joy in life.

It is also possible to use a variation of the body scan mediation from chapter 3 to check in with your energy levels on your own. By taking notice of the sensations in each area of your body, you can come closer in touch with any area of your body where you experience regular pain, tension, or other unpleasant feelings. This is often a sign of imbalance or trapped energy. Additionally, the tense and release technique in each area of the body can yield healing and balance by releasing negative energy and tension. It is important to check in with yourself daily, asking your body where energy may be trapped or depleted and what you can do to replenish yourself.

Chapter 3: The Daily Energy Healing Journey

Understanding Your Energy Field: Daily Energy Healing Meditation with Journaling (Week 5)

There is a great variety when it comes to human energy fields. People experience varying levels of sensitivity to the energy of other people and the environment. Some people are incredibly in tune with "vibes"; others are empaths who feel the emotional experiences of others on a deep level, while still others experience very little of either. There is also a lot of variation in the way people recharge energetically, as well as what depletes them. In the common case of introverts and extroverts, for example, introverts need time alone to replenish their energy and feel balanced, while extroverts recharge in stimulating environments with other people around. One of the first steps to protecting your personal energetic field is to understand how it works.

Understanding Your Energy Field Journal Prompt (Week 5):

When you feel exhausted and not like yourself, which activities are most likely to replenish your energy? Do you enjoy a night out with friends? Yoga? A walk in the park? Leisure reading? Finding a new adventure? Taking a bubble bath? Listening to your favorite music on blast? List 5-10 activities that help you gain balance and feel energized.

Now, make a list of the things that make you feel most drained. These can be large things, like a specific task at your job, or small things like doing the dishes. You may find that you feel drained if you spend too much time alone or, consequently, when you spend too much time around other people.

When it comes to activities that make you feel drained, ask yourself to what extent that specific thing is necessary in your life. If you find yourself feeling drained from spending too much time around other people, for example, you can easily make a change by scheduling more "nothing time" or "alone time" into your days and taking the time you need to replenish. Household tasks and daily responsibilities are necessary, but by being aware of the ones that drain you the most, you can bring more attention to the process and doing what you need to replenish energy before or after.

Protecting Your Energy Field: Daily Energy Healing Meditation with Journaling (Week 6)

Close your eyes and ask yourself, "what does my energy field look like?" Write down any specific colors, textures, shapes, or patterns of movement.

Once you have an image in your mind of your energy field, ask yourself, "What does it look like for outside energies to enter my field?" Write down what healthy and unhealthy outside energies look like.

Then ask yourself, "How can I regulate the energies entering my field? What does it look like when I decide what I will let in?" Describe this process.

Finally, ask yourself, "How does my body feel when I regulate what I allow to enter my energy field?" Write down everything that comes to mind.

Healing Through Trapped Emotion Release: Daily Energy Healing Meditation with Journaling (Week 7)

In our society, we are often faced with life circumstances that force us to repress our basic human emotions. It is very possible for anger, rage, or grief to become stuck in the body because it is considered "impractical" to have those reactions in public. Similarly, we often hear about people being described as "annoyingly happy" or "overly emotional." Most of us are taught not only to manage our emotions but to distance ourselves from them and react emotionally only in certain contexts. Additionally, we tend to suppress negative emotions such as fear, shame, inadequacy, and insecurity, for the purpose of appearing like we have everything together. Between life events and societal expectations, it is very easy for the emotions we suppress to become trapped in our bodies, which can create adverse health effects, negatively impact our relationships, and keep us from living our best lives.

Begin by making a list of as many emotions as you can think of

Run down the list of emotions one by one, asking yourself, "Is there anywhere in my body I am holding *particular emotion*?"

Write down the emotions you feel are trapped. Take some time to journal about how certain emotions arose, or times when you felt you had to suppress your emotions.

With each emotion you have labeled as being trapped, write: "I give myself permission to release this *particular emotion*

Cultivating Self-Trust in your Healing Journey: Daily Energy Healing Meditation With Journaling (Week 8)

No matter what you do in your life, there will always be people who don't understand the choices you make, or who judge the path you are on. When it comes to renewing and protecting your energy, there is no room for anyone else's opinions or emotions in regards to your journey. It requires a great deal of self-trust to go your own way and let what other people think about it roll off your back. For this reason, it is vital to begin everyday establishing a sense of self-trust with your own journey and energy management skills. The following four journal questions will help you direct your energy before going about your day.

What are you most grateful for today?

What are your intentions for how you will direct your energy today?

What are your fears/things you perceive as a potential threat?

What are your commitments to yourself and the world?

Mini Meditation Toolbox: 25 Quick and Easy Energy Restoration and Protection Meditations

One-Minute Energy Cleanse

- This meditation is useful if you find yourself with a person or in a specific situation that feels negative or energetically draining. You do not need to be alone to complete this meditation
- Pause where you are and allow yourself to take a few deep, cleansing breaths
- Focus exclusively on your breathing; you may close your eyes or leave them open
- Feel the inner power within the core of your body, around your abdomen. Remind yourself that you are in control and have the power to maintain balance.
- As you inhale, pull love, light, and peace into your body
- As you exhale, breathe out pain, annoyance, and toxicity

Energy from the Earth

- Begin by entering a space in nature. This can be on the beach, in the mountains, near a river, in a garden, by the lake, or in your own yard
- If possible, slip your shoes off, so your bare feet are in contact with the earth

- Start with a few cleansing breaths, taking note of everything you see, hear, smell, and feel in your environment
- Placing the soles of your feet on the ground, begin to breathe, pulling the energy from the earth up through your body
- Remember that you are One with the nature that courses around you. Allow it to heal what is broken within you and leave you feeling rejuvenated

Re-Centering Head Hold (3-5 minute meditation)
- Close your eyes and place the palm of one hand horizontally across the crown of your head, and the other palm across your forehead (over the energetic points of the Crown and Third Eye chakras). This position can be done while standing, sitting, or lying down.
- While clutching your head in this position, bring attention to any sensations in your body. What needs your attention most right now?
- Allow yourself to come back to the present moment, feeling grounded in your body and in your experience
- Breathe in awareness, focus, and comfort, exhaling anxiety and distraction
- When you open your eyes, notice how you feel grounded in your space

The Cloak of Protection

- This meditation is useful for energy protection before going out into the world, whether that is to work, the supermarket, an appointment, etc.
- Although you do not know what kinds of energies you may encounter, or which people may try to take your energy from you, remind yourself that you are in control of your own energy and that you have the capacity to protect yourself
- Close your eyes and imagine a dark-blue, almost black cloak made of a soft, thick material like a velvet night sky. The cloak is full-length with a hood to protect all of your chakras.
- Imagine a ray of light outlining the cloak in whatever color(s) feel most magical, protective, and authentic to who you are
- Set off into the world knowing that you are safe within yourself and your energy cloak and that you do not need to be afraid

De-Cluttering your Space

- When energy is lacking or out of balance, the spaces we live in are likely to reflect that imbalance with clutter and messiness. The more we feel like we "don't have our lives together," the more likely we are to have a messy desk, dishes piling up in the sink, laundry that still needs to be folded, or a car that has not been cleared of trash
- Such spaces do not allow for peace and mental clarity and can be even more draining to come back to after a long day

- Dedicate yourself to one area of your life to de-clutter. This can be your kitchen, your car, your bedroom, etc. Close your eyes before beginning and take a few deep, cleansing breaths to approach the task calmly
- Begin to address all of the clutter in the space, not only picking it up but putting it into a designated area where it can be organized and easy to find
- You may find that you want to create a special shelf or move some furniture around to make the space less cluttered. As you go, notice the energy that continues to unfold in your body
- When you finish, place a "clutter basket" in your room, the car, the living room, etc. where you can compile all the clutter throughout the day and put it away before bed

De-Cluttering your Mind (5-minute meditation)
- Close your eyes and begin to breathe deeply
- Ask yourself, "What is taking up the most space in my mind right now?"
- Bring your attention to whatever it is that is distracting you, and why it makes you feel out of control
- Breathe into that situation, saying, "I have control over this situation, and I am not going to let it spill out into the rest of my day. I am clearing this space."

The Energy-Ownership Mantra

- This meditation is ideal to perform in the morning, or before going out to interact with the world or other people
- Sit in a place where you feel energized (on the porch, in your meditation corner, etc.)
- Close your eyes and begin to breathe, checking in with any unresolved emotions or senses within the body
- Now begin to picture your energy field. Say to yourself: "My energy field is my sacred space, and other energies will only permeate it when I allow them to."
- Breathe into this thought for several moments
- Now, bring this thought into your mental space: "I have the wisdom to discern what belongs to me and what belongs to other people. I can be empathetic and attentive to other people's emotions, struggles, and opinions without assuming responsibility for them."

Epsom Bath Energy Renewal

- Begin by selecting your favorite scented Epsom salts. You may also customize your bath with petals, oils, and candles as according to the healing plants, herbs, and oils listed in Chapter 4
- Run a hot bath, letting your Epsom salts and other elements saturate the water
- Customize your space with the light of candles, meditative music, and anything else that makes you feel at peace

- Find a comfortable position inside the tub. Close your eyes, and feel your entire body relax into the heat and gentle movement of the water.
- Begin to conduct a body scan, feeling entirely vulnerable to this moment at peace with only yourself
- Ask your body, "What do I need right now?"
- The water should be hot enough that you begin to sweat (be sure to have a glass of water nearby). As you sweat, imagine your body purging itself of every blockage, every impurity, and every negativity

Sealing your Energy Field

- Close your eyes and begin to breathe
- Bring the image of your energy field to your mind. You may picture a wall, a bubble, or a glowing ring of light (this image may also differ depending on the day)
- Picture what other energies look like, floating around your field like particles in an atom. Say to yourself, "I am in control of what comes in."
- Imagine yourself recognizing people who are trying to take your energy or bear their burdens. Imagine any fear, anger, or resentment you may feel.

- Say to yourself, "No, not today." Imagine your bubble becoming impermeable, your wall being sealed, your glowing ring of light rejecting anything that does not belong inside
- Allow yourself to feel empowered over your energy, without feeling any resentment or judgment towards those who once posed a threat

Building your Sanctuary
- Sit down and close your eyes, beginning to breathe into yourself
- With each breath, ask yourself, "What makes me feel safe?" Repeat three times.
- Switch the phrase to "What makes me feel at peace?" Repeat three times.
- Switch the phrase to "What makes me feel loving?" Repeat three times
- Switch to "What makes me feel joy?"
- Lastly, ask yourself, "What makes me feel renewed?"
- When you ask yourself these questions, you may see certain crystals, scenes in nature, types of music, plants, aromas, decorations, activities, or color schemes. Take note of whatever comes to mind.
- Use these things that come to you in meditation to mindfully cultivate a space for yourself to come into every day when you need time to recharge. This can be a meditation corner, a spot in the

backyard, or any other space that is sacred to you and provides feelings of security and rest.

Cultivating Non-Reaction

- This meditation can be used when encountering a stressful situation, having a difficult conversation, or otherwise entering a state of nervous or angry energy
- Before responding to whatever the negative stimulant is, breathe into the moment. Close your eyes if needed.
- Tell yourself, "I can choose not to expend energy on this interaction. I can choose to move peacefully into the next moment."
- Feel the tension within you melt away as you make the choice not to internalize the stress of the situation or the negative energy coming at you

Boundary Setting

- Find a quiet place to sit and self-reflect. Breathe into the moment
- After you have settled into your breath, ask yourself, "What people, circumstances, or tasks drain my energy and leave me feeling agitated or exhausted?"
- Allow the answers to rise into your consciousness at will. Meditate on every name, every task, every circumstance which makes you feel tense and throws your energy out of balance.

- With each name, circumstance, and task, say to yourself, "This *person, place, thing* has no power over me. I can maintain my energy in spite of it."
- Next, ask yourself, "Where do I need to draw the line with this *person, place, thing*?"
- Listen to your intuition tell you what your boundaries should be. Perhaps, this looks like gently cutting off a toxic person, or limiting your interaction time with them. It could be quitting a job that is no longer good for you or asking for accommodations to make your environment more positive. It could be telling someone who expects you to bear their burdens that their energies are no longer your responsibility. Or, perhaps it is to establish a self-care activity to do directly after a draining task.

Trigger Awareness
- If your energy has ever been thrown out of balance by trauma, there are likely still factors of your environment that can strike at any time, causing your body to react in the same way it did at the time of the trauma.
- Breathe into the moment, asking yourself, "what elements of my environment cause me to lose control of my logic and feel afraid, helpless, irrational, in pain, or otherwise unbalanced or unhealthy energetically."
- These elements are called "triggers." Bring your awareness to these triggers, simply allowing them to be there without judgment.

- Say to yourself, "that moment in time is over. I can now release myself."

Energetic Tapping

- Begin by determining 3-5 affirmations or manifestations for the day ahead ("I manifest peace," "I am content," "I am present," "I manifest energy," "I am growing," "I manifest healing," "I manifest loving-kindness," etc.)
- Breathe deeply, pondering the affirmations/manifestations
- Choose your first manifestation/affirmation. With your index and middle fingers on both hands, begin tapping lightly on the crown of your head, repeating the manifestation or affirmation three times
- Move to the temples, tapping and saying the manifestation/affirmation three times
- Repeat at the inner corners of the brow bone
- Repeat just above the brow line
- Repeat at the top of the cheekbones
- Repeat below the ear lobes at the crest of the jawbone
- Repeat at the top of the chest
- Repeat on the left wrist, then switch to the right wrist
- Switch to the next affirmation/manifestation and go through the process again, staying in touch with your breath throughout

Listening to your Intuition
- Find a space where you feel completely comfortable and relaxed
- Begin to breathe deeply, coming into the present moment
- Ask yourself, "What does my inner self need me to know right now?"
- Keep breathing, holding space for whatever answer arises
- If necessary, you can ask follow-up questions to yourself, like "Is there any threat I need to be prepared to protect myself from?" or "How can I best love the world today?" Or "What do I need to do to take care of myself today?"
- Continue to breathe and hold space, trusting that your heart will guide you to make the correct decisions for yourself

Memory Reclamation (specifically for healing of trauma victims)
- Find a space where you feel totally safe and undisturbed. It is best to do this meditation on a day where you can invest in self-care and rest.
- Begin to breathe, telling yourself, "I am safe. I am safe. I am safe."
- Allow the memory of a particularly traumatic event to come to your mind. Continue to breathe, telling yourself, "I am safe."

- Pay attention to the details of that memory. What do you see? What do you hear? What do you feel?
- As the memory progresses, allow it to release its energetic hold on your body. Tell yourself, "That was then. This is now. I am safe."
- Feel the trauma release its hold on you, restoring itself to a basic memory of the past

Defining your Needs

- Sit in a peaceful place, breathing into the moment
- Bring attention to any pain or unrest within your body. Without judgment, allow it to be there, asking if there is anything you should learn from it.
- Generally, where there is pain or unrest, there is a need being left unmet. Ask yourself, "What is it that I need?"
- Allow your needs to arise into your consciousness ("I need a day off for my mental health," "I need a trip into nature," "I need a bath," "I need a warm, nourishing meal," "I need to go to sleep early," etc.)
- Breathe into each need, envisioning yourself meeting that particular need
- Ask yourself, "Is there anyone else I need to make aware of these needs?"
- Envision yourself having a calm conversation about your needs with your boss, your partner, your family, or a friend. Envision them, reacting gently and yourself feeling better understood and supported.

- Continue to breathe into your capacity to meet your energetic needs and make those needs known to others.

"Nothing Time"

- Set aside a minimum of one hour of time with absolutely nothing scheduled
- Sit down, breathing into the moment. Tell yourself, "this is my time. I have nowhere to be, nothing to do; I do not need to feel rushed."
- Allow your deepest intuition to guide your next step. Do whatever comes to mind first
- While you proceed with your "nothing time," allow your breath to guide every move

Discovering your Support System

- Bring your attention to the present moment, focusing on your breath
- Ask yourself, "Who of the people I know understands and embraces me for who I truly am?"

- Breathe with each name that comes up, allowing loving-kindness and appreciation for that person to flow through your body
- Ask yourself, "Who in my life encourages me to reach my full potential?
- Repeat the action of breathing with each name that arises
- Ask yourself, "Who in my life do I feel most at rest with?"
- Repeat the action of breathing with each name that arises
- Continue to breathe, saying to yourself, "These are my people. This is my support system. I will allow myself to lean on them when I need to."

Glowing Love-Energy

- Find a restful position and begin to breathe
- Imagine the aura of your energy field. How big is it? What color is it?
- Say to yourself, "I am pure love. I have room to love the entire universe and everything in it."
- Continue to repeat this phrase with every breath. Picture the aura expanding and glowing brighter

Jaguar Spirit Animal Protection

- Bring yourself into the present moment with deep breathing
- From the depth of your being, say, "I call on the spirit of the jaguar to protect me."

- Feel the reverberations of the jaguar's protection through your body, aiding you in repelling negative energy and toxicity
- Imagine a fierce, beautiful guard of your energy field, encircling you with fierce love and security

Energetic Breathing (1-3-minute meditation)
- Take some space away from your everyday life (in the bathroom, in the car, etc.) to just breathe
- Implement the 5-5-7 breathing technique
- With every breath in, say to yourself, "I breathe in pure energy."
- With every breath out, say to yourself, "I breathe out *exhaustion, *toxicity, *negativity, etc."
- Continue until you feel the tingle of pure energy coursing through your veins

Energetic Dancing/Movement
- Find a space where you can be alone and feel completely secure
- Play a song that stirs your soul and emotions, causing you to have a visceral reaction in the body each time you hear it
- As the song begins, close your eyes and deep breathe, maybe swaying back and forth slightly

- When you feel ready, release your body to move as it feels led. No choreography, no expectations, simply letting the movement of the moment lead your body into a state of pure surrender and release
- Surrender entirely to the moment, trusting your body to release any tension or trauma
- Give your body the space and freedom to heal, coming into energetic harmony

The Art of Saying "No"

- Close your eyes and begin to breathe deeply
- Begin to consider the things that drain your energy. Perhaps you have a tendency to overcommit or find yourself stuck in a relationship or circumstance that no longer serves you. Breathe with each of these places where you feel stuck
- Say to yourself "I have the power to say 'no.'"
- Imagine yourself having the necessary conversation, turning down the opportunity, or simply choosing to remove yourself from the situation
- Feel the power of saying no and being in full control of where you place your energy

The Restorative Power of Letting Go

- Breathe deeply, cultivating a sense of full peace and security
- Ask yourself, "Where are the parts of me that I need to get back?"
- Take notice of every person or place that comes to mind as still having a part of your energy and your essence
- If there are any feelings of melancholy, nostalgia, resentment, shame, or anger, allow them to be there, breathing as they flow through you
- Say to yourself, "I release this *person or place*. I reclaim what they have that is rightfully mine."
- Continue to breathe into this empowerment

PART III

Chapter 1- What is Self Compassion

What is the self-compassion? Have you thought about it or experienced it from someone?

The truth is, having compassion for yourself is not different from having compassion for other people or animals. Having self-compassion is being kind to yourself and understanding to your needs when you face personal failures. Think about how you would talk and console a friend who's going through a rough time- what would you say to them? Would you be harsh to them? Would you say things that bring them down even more?

The answers to those questions are of course a big NO. You would do what all good friends do- bring them up when they feel down, hug them and tell them everything is going to be ok, telling them that you'll be there for them to talk to or if they need help. Self-compassion is acting this same way towards yourself when you go through a rough patch. You notice the suffering and you empathize with yourself by comforting yourself, offering kindness and understanding.

Kristin D. Neff and Katie A. Dahm are two prominent are two names synonymous with the research on self-compassion. In their book, the Handbook of Mindfulness and Self-Regulation, it states that there are three primary components to self-compassion:

1. Self-kindness
2. Common humanity
3. Mindfulness

To understand self compassion, we need to consider what it means to feel compassion on a general level. Here are some views of compassion:

The Buddhist point of view of compassion is given to our own as well as to others suffering.

Goetz, Keltner & Simon-Thomans, 2010: Compassion is the sensitivity to the suffering that is happening, coupled with a deep desire to alleviate that suffering

Neff, 2003a: Self-compassion is compassion directed inwards, referring to ourselves as the object of concern and care when we are faced with an experience of suffering

The Three Elements of Self-Compassion

The key to understanding self-compassion is to understand the difference between this trait and more negative ones. Sometimes when we give ourselves self-compassion, it may be construed as narcissism to a point, which is why it is important to know what is self-compassion and to what degree is it considered self-compassion and when it isn't.

1. *Self-kindness is not Self-Judgement*

Self-compassion is being understanding and warm to ourselves when we fail, or when we suffer or at moments when we feel inadequate. We should not be ignoring these emotions or criticizing yourself. People who have self-compassion understand that being human comes with its own imperfections and failing is part of the human experience. It is inevitable that there will be no failure when we attempt something because failure is part of learning and progress. We will look into how failure is a friend in disguise in the next chapters. Having self-compassion is also being gentle with yourself when faced with painful experiences rather than getting angry at everything and anything that falls short of your goals and ideals.

Things cannot be exactly the way it should be or supposed to be or how we dream it to be. There will be changes and when we accept this with kindness and sympathy and understanding, we experience greater emotional equanimity.

2. *Common humanity and not Isolation*

It is a common human emotion to feel frustrated especially when things do not go the way we envision them to be. When this happens, frustration is usually accompanied by irrational isolation, making us feel and think that we are the only person on earth going through this or making dumb mistakes like this. News flash- all humans suffer, all of us go through different kinds of suffering at varying degrees. Self- compassion involves recognizing that we all suffer and all of us have personal inadequacies. It does not happen to 'Me' or 'I' alone.

3. *Mindfulness is not Over-Identification*

Self-compassion needs us to be balanced with our approach so that our negative emotions are neither exaggerated or suppressed. This balance act comes out from the process of relating our personal experiences with that of the suffering of others. This puts the situation we are going through into a larger perspective.

We need to keep mindful awareness so that we can observe our own negative thoughts and emotions with clarity and openness. Having a mindful approach is non-judgemental and it is a state of mindful reception that enables us to observe our feelings and thoughts without denying them or suppressing them. There is no way that we can ignore our pain and feel compassion at the same time. By having mindfulness, we also prevent over-identification of our thoughts and feelings.

Discovering Self Compassion

You're so dumb! You don't belong here loser! Those jeans make you look like a fat cow! You can't sit with us! It's safe to say we've all heard some kind rude, unwanted comments either directly or indirectly aimed at us. Would you talk like this to a friend? Again, the answer is a big NO.

Believe it or not, it is a lot easier and natural for us to be kind and nice to people than to be mean and rude to them whether it is a stranger or someone we care about in our lives. When someone we care is hurt or is going through a rough time, we console them and say it is ok to fail. We support them when they feel bad about themselves and we comfort them to make them feel better or just to give a shoulder to cry on.

We are all good at being understanding and compassionate and kind to others. How often do we offer this same kindness and compassion to ourselves? Research on self-compassion shows that those who are compassionate are less likely to be anxious, depressed or stressed and more resilient, happy and optimistic. In other words, they have better mental health.

Conclusion
It does make sense that people who have better self-compassion are happier and optimistic about their future. When we continuously criticise ourselves and berate ourselves, we end up feeling incompetent, worthless and insecure. This cycle of negativity continue to self-sabotage us and sometimes, we end up self harming ourselves.

But when our positive inner voice triumphs and plays the role of the supportive friend, we create a sense of safety and we accept ourselves enough to see a better and clear vision. We then work towards making the required changes for us to be healthier and happier. But if we do not do this, we are working ourselves towards a downward spiral or chaos, unhappiness and stress.

In the next chapters, we will look into the benefits of self-compassion, self-esteem, how to get rid of negative self-talk, mastering our emotions as well as practical exercises towards becoming self-compassionate.

Chapter 2- Benefits of Self-Compassion

You've probably heard your parents say time and time again to treat others as you would want them to treat you. Therefore, we are often taught to be empathetic and compassionate to others who are facing difficulties and challenges in their life. However, when faced with our own personnel challenges be it in our everyday lives, work and relationships, we often find ourselves becoming our own worst enemy. Hence we become too critical and judgmental on our own selves and in turn prevent any healing process from taking place.

Therefore, instead of being self-critical to oneself, we need to develop the concept of self-compassion in combating our negative thoughts and self-criticism that keeps us from overcoming our obstacles and challenges.

Self-compassion is defined as being compassionate to our own suffering, inadequacies, weakness and failures. As we know from the previous chapter, Kristin Neff, an associate professor at department of educational psychology in the University of Texas further breaks down self-compassion to 3 key elements which are self-kindness, common humanity and mindfulness.

Self-kindness is about recognizing our flaws and issues as well as being caring to oneself when going through bouts of hardship and challenges. Common humanity on the other hand, puts emphasis that the suffering and anguish we go through is all a natural part of being human and it's a normal part of everyday life. Lastly, mindfulness deals with the individual's ability to take a middle path in addressing their sufferings so as not to neglect or overthinking the situation.

Various research done on the topic of self-compassion indicates that individuals who practice self-compassion have a far greater psychological health than those who lack it. The individuals who practice self-compassion have a more positive life satisfaction, happiness and optimism. Apart from that self-compassion is also connected low levels of anxiety, self-criticism and depression. As such, in a way self-compassion can be used as a tool to develop inner strength when facing challenges in every aspect of our life.

So we know what self-compassion is and sure it helps us lead a better life and have better relationships. What other aspects of self-compassion are there? Here are some major benefits you can reap from being self-compassion. We explore it in terms of work, relationships and in life.

Self-Compassion At Work

Our daily work environment can be a long-lasting love-hate relationship with its own ups and downs that one has to face on a daily basis. As such, we are constantly bombarded with undue stress in meeting deadlines, reports and customer expectations. Many at times, we will face moments that completely overwhelm us and have a negative impact on us. This can be caused by numerous factors such as a negative remark by a colleague, superior or even a customer, failure to reach sales targets or goals, not getting that raise or promotion that you so deserve or even by making an unintentional mistake at the job. Since we all strive to achieve more and be perfect at our jobs, this negative circumstances will have an adverse effect if not dealt properly and swiftly.

Self-compassion can be used at work through the following means to reap various benefits: -

- Conducting a post-mortem to review the shortcomings and failures of a certain project or task and learning from these failures to prevent similar occurrences in the future.
- When facing criticism and rejection from colleagues, superiors and customers, instead of being self-critical and falling into complete despair, we will be able to be calm and focus our energies and thoughts of improving ourselves and not to allow stress to overwhelm ourselves.

- Applying self-compassion at work also helps us in being resilient through difficult scenarios especially is situations that we don't get a certain reward or promotion that we think we deserve.
- Self-compassion enables us to be more creative. When we fail a project or we do not complete a task or when a work event doesn't go as expected, being self-compassionate to ourselves will help us to look back at the series of events and instead of berating ourselves, we look back and see what we could have done better and learn from our mistakes. It makes us becoming more creative the next time around.
- Self-compassion builds trust. It enables you to be transparent and authentic, makes it easier for people to connect with you because you are your true self.
- Showing genuine compassion to yourself also means showing compassion to the people around you. When you show compassion to yourself, you extend this feeling to your co-workers and it makes them feel safe.
- Self compassion allows you to allow yourself and your team implicit permission to do their very best without worry of punishment or repercussions if something doesn't go right.

Self-Compassion In Relationships

In the topic of relationships be it a romantic or non-romantic relationship, we often find ourselves in situations of disagreement from time to time. And these can sometimes lead to moments of stress and unhappiness between oneself and their significant other/parent/sibling/friend. Self-compassion provides various ways much like our situations at work to help us deal with this issues and challenges. Many studies done on this matter point that self-compassion when used have the following positive impact on relationships: -

- Individuals who practice self-compassion know that every individual as well as themselves aren't perfect and are subjected to weaknesses and shortcomings
- They are able relate to their partners much better
- They are more warm and compassionate in understanding a situation
- They are more open to compromising to resolve a situation
- Individuals who are self-compassionate have better empathy. The bring out the best in their partners.
- They are more responsive and aware to the issues that their partner faces
- They are better listeners, they listen to understand and not answer
- People who practice self-compassion own up to their mistakes

Studies also have shown that individuals that lack self-compassion tend to have a negative effect on people around them which may lead to isolation. As such, those people who practice self-compassion have healthier and happier relationships and have a bigger a wide social circle.

Self-Compassion In Life

When encountering difficulties in daily life which can range from a number of issues/aspects such as health to financial issues, we need to act by being compassionate and kind to ourselves. When faced with various issues on a daily basis, self-compassion allows us to look for solutions to take care of oneself instead of berating or being overly critical of one's lack of accomplishments or weaknesses.

With that being said, an individual who practices self-compassion will look into various ways to engage their mind and body into healthy activities that can stimulate them and lets them focus on positive aspects instead of groveling on a negative situation. This can be in a form of an exercise, a hobby, prayer or even a warm bath or a cup of tea to calm themselves down.

Self-compassionate individuals tend to be more: -

- Happier
- Satisfied with life
- Resilient
- Emotionally intelligent
- Have better coping mechanisms
- Optimistic
- Creative
- Less judgemental
- Better goal-getters
- It greatly reduces mental problems

As such, cultivating the habits of self-compassion in every aspect of our life will allow to become the best version of ourselves and allow us to live much happier with the right mindset.

Chapter 3: Myths about Self Compassion

Many people do not have any issues with showing compassion to other people- it is a commendable quality. Compassion is often seen with kindness, tenderness, understanding, sympathy, empathy and of course the impulse to help those in need, whether human or animal.

However, with self-compassion, that is a different story altogether. For plenty of people, having self-compassion often relates to negative qualities such as self-serving, self-pity, self-centered, indulgent and just selfish. We seem to think that if we are not hard on ourselves or punishing ourselves over our failures and flaws, we risk a runaway ego and fall into the traps of false pride.

Take for example, Norman. A young bank executive who is also a new father. Between juggling work and a new baby, he also spends time volunteering as a football coach at a local shelter. He is a committed father and husband, a hard worker and a community role-model. But Norman has gone through several episodes of anxiety attacks simply because he feels overwhelmed, he feels he isn't contributing enough in his team at work and isn't good enough as a husband or father.

People have misgivings about self-compassion and it is only because nobody really knows what it looks like, or even how to practice it so it doesn't become excessive and borderline narcissistic. Self compassion has the element of mindfulness, of wisdom and the recognition to common humanity. Research by Kristin Neff points the myths that people have on self-compassion is the main reason why most of us are in the cycle of criticizing yourself over and over again. Here are the common myths:

#1 Self-Compassion is just a person crying out for self-pity
Let's get this straight- self compassion does not mean you are feeling sorry for

yourself. It is fact an antidote to self-pity. It isn't about whining about our bad luck but instead, self-compassion makes us more open to acknowledging, accepting and experiencing difficult feelings with the help of kindness. Self-compassionate people have a lower tendency of wallowing in self-pity about how bad the circumstances may be and this leads to better mental clarity and mental health.

Filip Raes of the University of Leuven conducted a study on the connection between self-compassion, mental health and ruminative thinking. This study was conducted among the students in his university. Students were first assessed using the Self-Compassion Scale developed by Dr. Kristin Neff. Participants were asked how often they responded to behaviors that corresponded with the main components of self-compassion. These behaviors included "I try to be patient and understanding towards the elements of my personality that I am not fond of"; "When things are going badly for me, I see them as part of life that happens to everyone".

The result of the study showed that students who had better self-compassion parameters were less whiny and broody when things did not go their way. They were also less anxious and less depressed and showed better signs of attentiveness.

#2 Self-compassion is a sign of weakness

Melissa, as a first born child was always seen as the responsible one, a label she has taken on with pride. She sees herself as a pillar of strength to her family. However, since Melissa got married, she has decided to take a step back and pay more attention to her new marriage. While her own family has never imposed on her, Melissa secretly feels as if she is not being a good daughter, and racked with guilt. When her friends suggested that she try not being too hard on herself, her reaction was to immediately tell them off, saying that self-compassion does not make her a good daughter. What Melissa does not know is that this is not a sign of her abandoning her family or a sign of weakness but discovering self-compassion is part of the process of resilience to us. When going through changes in life, self-compassion enables us to survive and thrive.

#3 Self-Compassion can make you a complacent person

Thinking that self-compassion makes you complacent is one of the biggest blocks you can place on yourself. It's so easy for us to criticize ourselves just because we fail to live up to certain standards and we immediately label ourselves as sloths. Do we do this to our kids too?

Amanda's daughter just failed her Biology test and upon finding out, Amanda starts berating her, saying that she is stupid and that she is ashamed of her. This is the exact same thing that Amanda tells herself when she fails to live up to a certain expectation. Rather than motivating her daughter, these comments on her daughter lose faith in herself and prevents her from trying to do better.

What Amanda can do however is practice a more compassionate approach to the situation by giving a hug, telling her daughter that it happens to anyone and what support can she give her daughter. Telling her daughter that she believes in her will help motivate her.

Amanda needs to give honest recognition to the failure as well as empathize with her daughter's unhappiness. This caring response helps us boost out self-confidence and spread emotional support.

While Amanda may not have said those words to her daughter, she still believes deep down that this type of negative feedback may spur her daughter to achieve the necessary goals. But thanks research on human emotions and its responses, showing self-compassion is more effective to boost a better rate of success than self-punishment.

Juliana Breines and Serena Chen of University of California conducted a research to examine the effects of self-compassion and to see how or if it was one of the factors that motivated participants to get involved in positive behaviors and make positive changes. Participants were ask to think back at a time when they felt guilty about such as lying to a partner, cheating in an exam which made them feel bad even till now. They were then randomly assigned to write to themselves from three different perspectives:

1. that of a compassionate and understanding friend
2. write about their own positive qualities
3. write about a hobby they enjoyed doing

Researchers found that participants involved in the self-compassionate perspective were more remorseful for their wrong doing and were more motivated to not repeat the offence.

The research concluded that self-compassion was not about evading personal accountability, rather strengthening it. Acknowledging our failures with kindness rather than judgements enables us to see ourselves clearly beyond the spectacles of self-judgement. Tell ourselves 'I can't believe I messed up. I got so stressed and I overreacted' rather than 'I cannot believe i said that. Why am I so mean?'

#4 Self-Compassions makes us more narcissistic

To many Americans, having high self-esteem means that you are special and beyond average. For some people with high self-esteem, the minute that we receive a less than average score, our self-esteem crashes and plummets. There is no way that everyone to be above average all the time. There are some areas that we can excel because we are naturally good at it but then there are aspects that we either under perform or we are just average. That is why diversity is good. At times when we do perform below average, we see ourselves like failures. The desire to be above average is always going to be there, as we like that feeling of high self-esteem. However this can make us be develop nasty behaviors.

Jean Twenge, a researcher from the San Diego University and Keith Campbell from the University of Georgia have been studying narcissism scores since 1987 among college students. It may not come as a surprise to you to know that among modern-day social media savvy students, narcissism ran high.

It is extremely important to note the difference between self-compassion and self-esteem. While they are both connected to our psychological well-being, the difference is very vivid:

- Self-esteem is evaluating your self-worth positively
- Self-compassion is relating to the changes that happen to us with kindness and acceptance

With self-esteem, we want to feel better than the people around us but with self-compassion, we acknowledge the fact that we have and share certain imperfections. Self-esteem is buoyancy, depending on our latest success or failure. Those with higher levels of self-esteem tend to get upset when they receive neutral feedback. They often start thinking 'Am I just average? I thought i was exceptional'. They are also likelier to listen to any feedback that is related to their personality and blame it on external factors. Self-esteem thrives only when the reviews are good which leads to evasiveness.

Self-compassionate people on the other hand are more emotionally stable despite the degree of praise they receive.

#5 Self-compassion makes us selfish

It is easy to conflate self-compassion with selfishness. Joshua for example spends a large portion of his day caring for his family and at weekends, he supports activities at the local college. He was raised in a family placed importance on service to others. This eventually led him to think that spending time for self-care and being kind and caring to his needs meant he must be neglecting the people around him just for his own needs.

There are plenty of people like Joshua- selfless, good, altruistic and generous to others but horrible to their own selves. When we become too absorbed in self-judgement, we end up giving less because we are preoccupied by thinking about our inadequacies and worthless selves.

Plenty of our emotional needs are met when we are kind and nurturing to ourselves which leaves us in a better position to focus on the people around us. However, caring for the welfare of others often becomes a bigger priority and the idea of treating ourselves badly starts rearing its ugly head. Think about the safety message on an airplane. It is advised to place the oxygen mask over your ownself before assisting others right? This is the same for self compassion.

Kristin Neff conducted a research with Tasha Beretvas of the University of Texas just to prove that being good to ourselves is more helpful when we want to be good to others. The research look at whether people who were self-compassionate were more giving in their relationships. It explored 100 couple who are in romantic relationships for a year or longer. Participants were asked to rate themselves based on the Self-Compassion Scale.

Neff & Beretvas found that partners who were self-compassionate individuals were described as more accepting, caring and supportive compared to self-critical partners who were seen as detached, controlling and aggressive. Self-compassionate partners brought to the table a more secure and satisfied relationship.

A growing research also focuses on therapists and caregivers who were more self-compassionate. Those who were were less likely to feel caregiver burnout and they were more satisfied with their careers, they were more happy, they felt more energized and were more grateful to be able to make a difference.

Conclusion

Self-compassion enables us to feel love, courage, wisdom and generosity in a more sustainable way. It gives us a boundless and directionless mental and emotional state. The power of self-compassion can be enriched through practice and of course through learning, just like so many other good habits.

Being kind to ourselves is not a selfish luxury or a sign of weakness or self-pity. It is a gift to our persons to make us happier and more fulfilled. Thanks to the many research conducted, we now know the myths of self-compassion.

Chapter 4- Dealing with Negativity

Did you ever realize that it is much easier to be happy than it is to be unhappy? Go ahead. Think about it. While you are reading this, just think about the many things that happened before you opening this book and reading. What happened when you woke up? Did you get a kiss from your partner? How did your coffee taste this morning? How is the weather outside like now? All these things that happened to you today, what made you happy and what made you sad?

If you listed ten things today and 7 of them were things that made your happy and three made you unhappy, sad, frustrated or moody, then most likely you were grateful, and you were positive. The thing is, many of us would prefer to be happy and positive rather than be unhappy and negative. And it is that simple to be positive and happy. Also, positive thinking is above and beyond just being happy or displaying a cheerful and upbeat attitude. It also creates and establishes value in your life and relationships, and it also helps you build skills that benefit you longer than your smile can take you. Barbara Fredrickson, a positive psychology researcher from the University of North Carolina, published a landmark paper on the impact of positive thinking on work, health and general wellbeing. Here's a little brief of Barbara's research:

What Can Negative Thinking do to your Brain?
Our brain is programmed to respond to negative emotions by shutting off the world around us and limiting the options we see around us. For example, if you get into a fight with your sister, your emotions and anger might consume to the point where you react adversely- you can't think about anything else. Or for instance your coffee this morning spilled on your shirt, and this creates a domino effect of everything going wrong in your day, and you get so stressed out that you find it hard to start or do anything because you've lost your focus. Or if you are supposed to complete a project but you didn't, you start to feel bad about it and

all you think is how irresponsible you are and that you are lazy, and you lack motivation. The point is, our brain shuts off from the outside world and relies on the negative emotions of fear, stress, and anger. Negative thoughts and emotions prevent us from seeing other options, solutions or choices that are around us.

What Can Positive Thinking do to your Brain?

Barbara Fredrickson also explains how positive thinking manifests in our brain. She explains with an experiment where research subjects are divided into five groups, and each group is shown a different video clip. The first group was shown clips that created feelings of joy whereas the second group was shown clips that created contentment, the third was the control group that had images of no significant emotions and were neutral whereas group four had clips that created fear and group five had clips that created the feelings of anger.

Participants were then asked to imagine themselves in situations that these same emotions would come about and write down their reactions to it. Participants that viewed images of fear and anger had the least responses or reactions whereas participants who saw joy and contentment had more reactions. The bottom line is, if you experience positive emotions you will see more possibilities in life. Positive emotions broaden our possibilities and thinking, thus opening up more options for us in facing issues, crisis, problems, and solutions and so on. In the next few chapters, we will discuss how we can work our mind to be more positive and look at things in a more positive perspective to enhance and give more value to our life, relationships, and goals. It is not as hard as it seems because all it takes is a little practice.

Have you seen the movie Inside Out?

If you did, then you will probably realize that being sad is a good thing- not always, but this emotion is there for a reason. When we talk about dealing with negativity, it doesn't necessarily mean being optimistic all the time, especially in the face of suffering.

Pain and sadness are just part of the complex human emotions all of us have, and it is just as important to feel pain and sadness, guilt and fear as this are all part and parcel of coping. Experiencing and processing negative emotions in a healthy way is a crucial part of personal growth.

There are two scenarios when people are confronted with negative situations. One, they either obsess over the problem or two, they numb their emotions. Either of these coping methods is not healthy, and it can create harmful patterns in our mind, over a period of time. Obsessing is deceptive because it feels as if you are thinking things through but to continuously obsess over a situation only reinforces the impact of the negative thoughts and emotions.

That said, numbing your emotions towards a pained situation isn't good either because it really is not possible to selectively numb out an emotion. Humans are so complex that our range of emotions does not enable us to directly shut down an emotion. If you somehow blot out anger, you'll blur out happiness and serenity too. Why? Because while you like being active and optimistic all the time, not showing anger to something that has hurt you or pained you or frustrated you, will make you feel more bitter eventually. Only because you weren't able to express your anger, the situation or the person related to this will not know how you feel. For example, if we use alcohol to numb our pain, we do not learn how to cope with sadness. We just develop another problem which is alcohol abuse.

If you are going through a pained time, then you need to develop healthy coping skills, and this involves recognizing the inevitability and necessity of some suffering and moving on from it. The process usually includes:

- Acknowledging your negative feelings and watch them with a non-judgmental attitude

- Recognize when they are triggered and assess your reactions when responding to this
- Understand that pain is just a catalyst for growth and resilience
- Practice forgiveness towards those who have pained you
- Express yourself in creative and healthy ways like painting or exercising
- Seek the support of others

Steps to deal with Negative thoughts and Events

Here are some tried and tested ways to overcome negative thoughts and events which you can try:

1. Meditate or do yoga.

Yoga helps take your focus away from your thoughts and bring attention to your breath. Yoga or meditation is very relaxing, and it helps ease one's mind. It also helps you stay present and focused on the moment that is happening.

2. Smile.

Pain and sadness can make it very hard to smile. While it does seem hard to smile when you aren't feeling so happy inside, you need to sometimes force this out of you. So try doing this in front of a mirror everyday or make a mental note to smile to the people you correspond with daily.

3. Surround yourself with positive people.

Surround yourself with friends and family that can give you constructive and loving feedback. Each time you feel you are going down into your negative spiral, call these people up and speak to them so they can put your focus back again to where it's needed to be at the time.

4. Change your thoughts from negative to positive.

Easier said than done, no doubt but you can turn any situation into a positive one. For example, if you have just started a new job you barely have enough experience of, instead of saying 'I'll take a long time to adjust or learn' just say 'I will take on any challenges because challenges excite me!'

5. *Don't wallow in self-pity. Take charge of your life*

You are the captain of your shop so do not make yourself a victim. There is always a way out of any situation so if it becomes to unbearable, then leave. Otherwise, you stay put and make the best of it and don't point fingers, blame, complain or whine.

6. *Volunteer*

Volunteering also takes the focus away. If you think you are in a bad situation, imagine the people who need food aid or money. Do something nice for someone else so volunteer at an organization or donate.

7. *Remember to keep moving forward*

We easily dwell on our mistakes and feel terrible for the way we acted. But you can't reverse the situation so instead of feeling sorry for yourself or beating yourself up over what you'd done, tell yourself that you'd made a mistake, you learned from it, and you want to move on.

8. *Listen to music*

One of the best ways to alleviate your mood especially in the morning is by listening to songs and singing in the shower! It doesn't matter if you remember the lyrics – a good happy song will put you in a good and happy mood.

9. *Be grateful*

Being grateful enables you to appreciate all the things you have. So be grateful every day.

10. Read positive quotes.

Just log into Pinterest, read positive quotes every day. Better yet, print out the ones that you like and stick in on your wall, your fridge or your computer.

Learn to Forgive Yourself

Just like negative emotions, failure is also good to experience because it only makes us stronger.

Yes! Failure is something that didn't kill you. You're still alive! So what doesn't kill you only makes you stronger. Why do you need experience failure? Nobody wants to experience failure but if you looked at the successful people in our generation today, or even the past- they all failed. They all made mistakes. They all went through trial and error. What sets them apart from the perennial failures? They didn't give up. They learnt from their mistakes. They had extreme passion, making them eager to keep on trying till they succeeded. Here's why you need to experience failure:

Without failure, you'd be sucked into a blissful feeling that nothing can go wrong and that everything you'd put into place will work exactly as how it should be

When something does go wrong, you are unable to cope with the change or adapt to create solutions.

Failure enables us to work on our flaws and it also allows us to right our wrongs. Failure also enables us upgrade or enhance or refine our work, technique and solutions

Failure also teaches us a lesson. It is our choice to learn from it or run from it

When we fail, it's easy to get discouraged and upset and we develop a sense of being afraid to fail again. In order to be successful in anything that we do, we just need to remind ourselves to let go of our pride and ego. Failure only makes us grow wiser, make us more adaptable and vivid to any possible scenarios that could happen. We are more prepared to face the same problem but at a different angle.

So how do you look at failure at a positive way? We need to redefine the way we view failure. The fear of failure is what stops many great individuals from creating something beneficial and meaningful in our world. The fear of failure is why we stop ourselves from living extraordinary lives.

The fear of failure is why we never submitted the novel we wrote, we never expressed our feelings to the people we love, never bungee jumped or telling someone how you really feel.

Daniel Epstein, founder of Unreasonable group stresses the point of re-branding the way we see failure. He suggests defining it as such:

"To Fail means "to not start doing something you believe in. To stop doing something you believe in just because it is hard. To ignore your gut instinct around what you believe is right and wrong."

In actual fact, many of the world's greatest philosophers, entrepreneurs, scientists and artisans have all expressed their thoughts on failure and how it has helped them overcome adversity and obstacles. All these perceptions tell us that fear of failure is evident in every human being but with passion and perseverance to achieve what you want will be the driving force in the determination between constant failure and success.

Hopefully, these quotes will give you a good perspective. After all, what better way to learn than to be inspired by some of the most successful people on earth?

Remembering that I'll be dead soon is the most important tool I've ever encountered to help me make the big choices in life. Because almost everything – all external expectations, all pride, all fear of embarrassment or failure – these things just fall away in the face of death, leaving only what is truly important. ~Steve Jobs

I've missed more than 9000 shots in my career. I've lost almost 300 games. 26 times, I've been trusted to take the game winning shot and missed. I've failed over and over and over again in my life. And that is why I succeed. ~Michael Jordan

Our doubts are traitors, and make us lose the good we oft might win, by fearing to attempt. ~William Shakespeare

For every failure, there's an alternative course of action. You just have to find it. When you come to a roadblock, take a detour. ~Mary Kay Ash

Failure is blindness to the strategic element in events; success is readiness for instant action when the opportune moment arrives. ~Newell D. Hillis

The only real failure in life is not to be true to the best one knows. ~Buddha

Success is often achieved by those who don't know that failure is inevitable. ~Coco Chanel

Steps to Overcome Failure

Highly successful people are the ones who have failed the most. We only hear about their successes but never the trials and tribulations and obstacles that they had to go through. Setbacks and failures are part of life and nobody is perfect. Yes we fall into hard times at some point in our lives but what this is all a lesson to us. If we can manage it effectively, then no matter what comes our way in the future, we can overcome it. Here are four steps that can help you turn any negative experience into a positive one:

- **Failure is part of the road to success**

When times get tough, the tough get going. It is frustrating to hear people tell us to be positive when we are faced with adversity but this doesn't mean we have to be smiling all the time or be happy all the time. Staying positive is knowing that despite your setback, you can bounce back again. Staying positive is learning and growing and evolving. Understand that setbacks aren't the end of the road; rather it is carving a step in our journey to succeed. When life hits you with a setback, its okay to be sad and frustrated and upset- but we should never stay down.

- **Blow your Steam off**

When you hit a setback or a failure, your mind gets clouded. You worked so hard to get to this point, only to fail. If you have come to this point, take a step back and evaluate your work. Take some time off to clear your head and accept your mistakes. Once you have done this, you will begin to accept what has happened and how it happened or why it happened. This emotional state will eventually evaporate and then you can go back to focus on the work at hand.

- **Be Honest**

Being brutally honest to ourselves in the midst of a failure is a trait of success. Most people do not want to admit their mistake or admit that it is their own fault that all these negative scenarios have happened. The thing is, part of being positive is also about being responsible and being accountable to ourselves and the mistakes we have made. We need to do this because this is how we learn. Albert Einstein once said that it is crazy to keep doing the same thing over and over again and expecting different results. That is why learning from our mistakes is a crucial part of moving on and part of learning. If we do not learn from our mistakes, we are doomed to be repeating them again and again and again.

- **Move Forward**

We need to move forward each time we fail. When we fail, we fail forward which means learning from our setbacks and then, making the necessary adjustments until we reach success. You have come so far, do not give up. So each change we make, each person we meet and every tiny bit of information we learn all combines to create a different outcome for us to learn from.

Obstacles are inevitable in life but there are always two ways of handling them. While they may block your focus out temporarily, our perseverance is the element that determines whether we fall back or move forward. As we get more and more efficient in the journey of positive thinking, we will enable ourselves to always see the positive side of things even in the most darkest of situations or the hardest of times.

Surrounding yourself with Positive People
No doubt that people have a huge impact on your life. According to Jim Rohn, American entrepreneur and motivation speaker, we all spend our time with an average of five people. With this in mind, think about who these 5 people are and how they impact your life.

Some people, including your friends whom you've known for a long time, can be parasites. These parasites suck out your energy and happiness and even your resources.

So what makes someone a 'good' person you can spend your time with? What are the benefits of surrounding yourself with self-disciplined people?

Your GOOD Category
The people around you can be good in so many ways. This doesn't mean that

they go to church every Sunday. It's more like feeding the poor, looking after abandon dogs or something simple like encouraging you to hit the gym more often. These people can be your friends, your family, your co-workers and even some acquaintances.

In essence, good people are productive people. They have a lot of good traits in them that inspire and motivate you too.

It is also important to note too much of something good can also inhibit your growth. You need diversity and healthy arguments and discussions along the way. Always be eager to learn new knowledge and look at different perspectives from your peers.

Think About How You Interact with People

Time for a little exercise. Write down the names of the five people you usually spend time with. Then, write down the qualities you see in them. Think about how they positively or negatively affect you. Are you happy around them? Do they make you feel like you got what it takes to reach your goals? Do they support you? If your list has more positives than negatives, then you probably have the good people around you.

You want to surround yourself with people who make you happy, with those that make you feel alive, the people who help you when you are in need and those that make you feel safe- they are the ones who genuinely care and are worth keeping in your life.

The key here is to finding what is good for you because what is good for you may be different for someone else.

So how do you do that?

Your vibe is what will attract the people around you. When you give off good vibes, good vibes will follow you. You will also feel less stressed and find joy even in the most simplest things like the blue sky or a scoop of vanilla ice cream.

So train your mind to not think negatively and try to see the positive side of things. It is ok to feel sadness and grief and bitterness when things don't go the way you want or something bad happens but if you start building a home in the negativity scene, it'll be harder for you to leave it.

Today, make a commitment to start spending more time with the good people in your life.

Benefits of surrounding yourself with Positive People
1. You Do not get into needless battles

Thoughts become things- you've heard it before. But some of these things are also feelings and feelings are energy. The feelings of happiness, sadness, gratitude, confidence are all energy- negative and positive. When you surround yourself with positive people, you eliminate negative energy, thus eliminate unnecessary conflicts.

You get to live in the feeling of gratitude more frequently

People who are happy will genuinely be happy for you when you make it big or achieve your goal. Surrounding yourself with unsuccessful people and then talking about your successes will only remind these people of what they don't have. By contrast, surrounding yourself with people that have more than what you have you will make you feel more gratitude frequently. Gratitude is the attitude that brings success.

For example, if you achieved your goal in achieving a healthy, physically toned body, you're not going to be telling this to someone who is overweight (by choice) right? Because that person will only think you are bragging and wont share in your good fortune.

2. You get to be someone you've never been

In order to do something you have never done before, you need to stop caring about what people think of you. You need to realize that you cannot be doing the same things you have done if you want to become someone better. Surrounding yourself with people who want to achieve the same goal as you can make you do things you otherwise will not do. Successful people recognize that change is inevitable and that it must take place. Unsuccessful people will begrudge the changes in you whereas successful people will be glad that it happened and welcome it.

Chapter 5: Building and Mastering Emotions

Being aware of our emotions also means knowing that our emotions can drive our behavior and impact those around us, either positively or negatively. It also means we have the ability to manage these emotions, that of our own and that of others, especially at pressuring and stressful times.

The Five Categories of Emotional Intelligence (EQ)

When it comes to Emotional Intelligence, there are five categories that becomes a focus.

1. **Self-awareness.**

Having self-awareness means having the ability to recognize an emotion as and when it occurs and it is the key to your EQ. In order to develop self-awareness, a person needs to tune into their own true feelings, evaluating them and subsequently managing them.

In self-awareness, the important elements are:

- Recognizing our own own emotions and its effects
- Having a level of confidence and sureness of your capabilities and your self-worth

2. **Self-regulation.**

When we experience emotions, we often have little control over our actions when we first feel these emotions. One thing we can control however is how long these emotions last. To control how long certain emotions last, especially negative ones, certain methods are used to lessen the effects of these emotions such as anxiety, anger and even depression. These methods include reinventing a scenario in a much positive manner such as through taking a long walk, saying a prayer and even meditating.

Self-regulation includes:
- Innovation which means open to new ideas
- Adaptability to handle change and be flexible
- Trustworthiness referring to the ability to keep to standards of integrity and honesty
- Taking responsibility, conscientiousness of our own actions
- Self-control to prevent disruptive impulses

3. **Motivation**

Having motivation is what keeps us going to accomplish our tasks and goals and to maintain an air of positivity. With practice and with effort, we can all program our minds to be more positive although as human beings, it is also good to be negative at times. This does not mean having negative thoughts are bad, but these thoughts need to be kept in check as they cause more harm than good. Whenever you feel like you have negative feelings, you can also reprogram them to be more positive or at least to pick out the positive aspects of the situation, the silver lining which will help you be more focused in solving the problem.

Motivation is made up of:
- Having the sense of achievement drive, to constantly strive to improve and meet a level of excellence.
- Having the commitment to align your individual, group or organizational goals
- Having the initiative to act on available opportunities
- Having the optimism to pursue your goals persistently and objectively, despite the setbacks and obstacles.

4. **Empathy**

Empathy is the ability to recognize how people would feel towards a certain scenario, thing or person. Having this ability is crucial to success both in career as with life. The more you can decipher the feelings of people, the better you can manage the thoughts and approaches you send them. Empathetic people are excellent at:

- Recognizing, anticipating and meeting a person's needs
- Developing the needs of other people and bolstering their individual abilities
- Taking advantage of diversity by cultivating opportunities among different people
- Developing political awareness by understanding the current emotional state of people and fostering powerful relationships
- Focusing on identifying feelings and wants of other people

5. Social skills.

Developing good interpersonal skills is imperative as well if you want a successful life and a successful career. In our world today when plenty of thing are digitized, social skills seem to be an afterthought. People skills are more relevant and sought-after then before especially since now you also need a high EQ understand, negotiate and empathize with others especially if you deal and interact with different people on a daily basis. Among the most useful skills are:

- Influence to effectively wield persuasive tactics
- Communication to send our clear and concise messages
- Leadership to inspire and guide people and groups.
- Change catalyst in kick-starting and managing change
- Managing conflicting situations which includes the ability to negotiate, understand and resolve disagreements

- To bond and nurture meaningful and instrumental relationships
- Teamwork, cooperation and collaboration in meeting shared goals
- Creating a synergetic group to work towards collective goals.

Creating a Balance with Emotional Awareness

As a human being, emotions and feelings make up every aspect of our existence. Managing them and keeping them balanced will help us reach our maximum potential in life, at work and especially in our relationships. As we know by now, having good emotional balance leads us towards better physical and mental health, making life happier.

When our emotional well-being is disrupted, this will result in the opposite. Our physical health will decline, we will start having digestive problems, lack of energy and sleep issues. People with emotional distress often exhibit low self-esteem, they are self-critical and pessimistic. They always need to assert themselves through their behavior. They are overly worried, get afraid very fast and they are focused on the past.

- Connection between our Thoughts and Feelings

Thoughts determine our feelings and they are nothing more than firing the neurons in our body. Our thoughts also generate feelings, making our body release additive natural substances such as cortisol and adrenaline.

The connection between the body and the mind is extremely vivid and strong, strong enough that the mental and physical state sends positive and negative vibes both ways. The feelings we experience depends on our thought, combined with our attitudes and actions.

Emotions are part of our daily life and we experience this everyday. What we want is to strike a balance in our emotions, thoughts and feelings to ensure that they do not adversely affect our daily tasks and cause us stress.

- **Creating Emotional Balance**

So how we do create emotional balance? Emotional balance is the ability to maintain equilibrium and flexibility between the mind and body when we are faced with changes or challenges. Here are some ways that you can create emotional balance:

1. **Accept your emotions**

Many of our mental, emotional and physical problems stem from our inability to express ourselves emotionally. When we experience an emotional distraught, we smother it in the comforts of eating, sleeping, sweating it out, sucking it up, it is swept under a rug, we bury it, project it elsewhere, meditate even all in the hopes of suppressing our emotions instead of actually dealing with it by accepting that this is what we are going through right not. The key here is to allow ourselves unconditional permission to feel- to cry when we want to, to feel anger when we are angry, sadness when we grief and so on. Let your guard down either when you are alone or with someone you trust and just focus on the feeling and situation. Experience and immerse yourself in this feeling so you can comprehend better why it hurts and what you will be doing to remedy the situation once you've accepted and acknowledge these feelings.

2. **Express yourself**

Expressing yourself is important. There are many ways to express oneself and usually when we experience a feeling, we react by crying, shouting, throwing things. But to identify with ourselves and be able to manage our emotions properly, we can also express ourselves through more positive ways. Some people like reading as it provides an escape into a different world. Some people express themselves through art or music. Whatever it is that you do, make sure you stay connected to discover more about yourself, your identity and also the person you want to become.

3. Don't shove your feelings

Sometimes, it is easy to shove our feelings and not think about it, especially painful and scary memories. But as we all know, stuffing your memories and feelings will only make things worse for you. While it is hard to address your fears and sadness, rage and anger, once you actually dive into it, you will find that it will become easier to face your fears and eventually, the choppy waters will become calmer.

Be accepting your past and dealing with it in a more emotional state, you ultimately will lead a harmonious life. Always allow yourself to feel because your reactions to these different feelings would be in a more stable way rather than an overreaction.

4. See the world in a positive light

It is easier said than done, we know. In a world full of hatred, sadness, grief, war, crime, unfairness- it is a threat to our emotional health. You tend to develop low self-esteem and start asking yourself if you are worth it, if you can get through it, if you are doing things right and all these thinking steers you towards making more mistakes and missteps. Rather than having emotional self-doubt, take action to develop a prerogative of seeing the world in a more positive light.

Do not feel responsible for the bad things that happen which is not caused by you is a good start. Have compassion in yourself and practice mindfulness and accept that occasional lapses and failures are just part of being human.

5. Get a grip on your mind

The way we think causes us emotional distress- this probably is not news to you.

We all have this tendency into overthinking and these thoughts that do not serve you or give you any positivity is just setting you up for emotional distress. So get a grip on your mind- do not let it wander to much especially when you start overthinking.

6. Practice Yoga and Mindfulness

Doing yoga on a daily basis does help in your mental health- it helps by increasing your confidence in your abilities and it also helps you make better, definitive decisions.

You also learn to not be so self-criticizing. Yoga, practiced on a daily basis can help get rid of negative energy within you and help you work your way towards mental clarity and vital energy.

Not only that, the breathing that is practiced in yoga helps you relax better, make you calmer especially if your mind is racing and it also helps you to refine your feelings.

Breathing correctly helps you get rid of stress and anxiety as well.

Conclusion

While emotional balance is vital, just remember that it is alright to have emotional imbalance so do not beat yourself up over it and overthink things. However, do not neglect this imbalance. If you feel you are emotionally imbalanced, do something about it either talk to someone you trust, meet a therapist or just find a positive way to express your emotions and feelings. Live a life without or little regrets.

Chapter 6: Practical steps for Becoming self compassionate

Self-compassion is necessary for a healthy relationship, healthy mind and healthy body. How we interact with people and how we think affects how our body responds too. Self-compassion is the practice of goodwill and not good feelings. To practice self-compassion, we have first and foremost, change the way we think and perceive things. We also need a little bit of faith and believe in ourselves, in our strengths, in the way our life is heading, our goals and our priorities.

In this chapter, we will look at:

- the power of faith and believe in changing our perceptions
- practising creative visualization
- Practising affirmations

- **Faith & Believe**

When someone says 'Have faith' this depends on what you view or think what faith is. For many people, faith can be many different things and in all honesty, there's no right or wrong.

Conventionally, a lot of people associate faith with spirituality or the faith in God and that's not wrong either but like mentioned above, the very fact that people have different perspectives of what faith is is a good thing! It is quite enlightening and helpful to plenty of individuals that faith has different meanings as it can help different people make clearer sense of the various spectrums of life.

Here's a quick guideline to what faith means:

- **Faith**

Faith can mean faith in a supreme being, in God. But psychologists of religion would say that this is more of belief. Faith, in a more naturalistic and psychological sense, is really about the innate sense to search for meaning, purpose, and significance. Every human person has a strong sense that there is more than what meets the eye. In other words, there is something more than just 'me' and as human beings, we all discover what this might be- some of us go all out while some of us are content with the information we have at the moment.

All of us human beings seek out to find the deeper meaning, purpose and significance that exist in our lives, in our relationships and all the things that occur around us. This is the very basic striving of faith and the universal role it plays in our lives.

Wikipedia describes faith as a trust or confidence on a person, element or thing. Faith also is connected to the observation of an obligatory process that creates loyalty or even fidelity to a person, a promise or engagement. Faith is also a belief that is not based on facts and proof and faith can also mean loyalty to a system of religious belief.

While we think that only people that belief in divine intervention or God seem to have faith, the thing is even atheists have this kind of faith- a belief or trust or confidence. Everyone has the gift of faith- some of us have strong faith while some of us have weaker faith, but it really depends on the context we talk about.

- Belief

This brings us to the next element- belief. Belief is a representation of truth claims that you make on your spiritual journey. Beliefs are what tell you what is true and what is not true, and this is based on your experiences to satisfy your sense of faith. Your beliefs are what your hold to be true in your journey to satisfy your faith by engaging in various spiritual pursuits such as pilgrimage.

- **The Value of Faith**

While we all like to think we have faith (and high levels of it) the truth is, the value of our faith only grows when we are faced with troubling times. Many people believe that their faith value is determined by the evidence of things or successful moments or achievements in life. But the value of faith only increases as we grow older, as we experience more and more things in life, some good and some bad. Our faith becomes more valuable as we go through the trials and testaments of life and its heartaches. It is only during these times that you truly understand the depth and strength of a person's faith.

- **The Difference between Faith & Belief**

Probably by reading this now, you'd come to deduce that faith and belief are not the same things. In fact, in most cases, faith and belief are entirely the opposite of each other. Confusion between these two elements is tested when you face a crisis. While you may be searching for faith in something at a moment of crisis, you may be only pulling out the various beliefs that you have.

So the question is, who are you if not for your convictions?

If you have gone through a terrible crisis in life, you are probably still trying to figure it all out. Some people take years to understand why what happened to them, happened. Many people, especially those who are religious, feel the need to leave their faith in God because they believe that God has abandoned them.

But the questions are, were you abandoned by God or were you abandoned by your beliefs?

- **Belief as a product of the Mind**

A negative mind is already at a disadvantage but even a healthy mind can run into its own set of problems. For the enabled mind, a person may think that because they pray to God, all their prayers will be answered and that God is just and he will set things right. The positive mind will say that if we hold on to our beliefs strongly, God listens and will favor us.

But what is it that we believe in? Our beliefs are rooted in our culture and our upbringing. This is the first thing that separates our faith from our belief. Oftentimes, what we belief in may directly contradict everything else we know to be true and right. It can be universally acknowledged that we arrive at the crossroads of faith and belief when we go through a life-threatening crisis ourselves and when this happens, we end up changing our stronghold beliefs.

Changing our minds to adapt to crises is to change some part or elements of our beliefs. It is perfectly normal to shift our beliefs because our beliefs are modeled on personal and communal experience. A belief can necessarily be not true even when it has been handed down to us. In other words, a belief is not necessarily the only truth.

- **Belief is a product of the mind, faith is not**

Faith is the product of the spirit. Our mind also has a tendency to interfere with the process of faith rather than contributing it. To have confidence in the most depressing of times will require us to quiet the mind because the mind can run amok when we let it, especially when we have every negative thought clouding our mind.

Faith comes in when our beliefs run aground. Be wary that our beliefs can sway our spirit. Think of Galileo and how everyone thought the world was flat until he came around to prove that the world was indeed round. The belief that we humans have held for centuries can come and go over the course of a millennium.

- **Beliefs come and go**

But our faith is not as fickle as our belief. True faith is not a statement of our beliefs, but it is a state of being. Faith is trusting beyond all reasonable doubt and beyond all evidence that you have not been abandoned. Faith is achieved through commitment and to commit to faith is not the same thing as committing to a series of beliefs. When we are in the moment of crisis, faith tells us it doesn't matter whether its God or circumstances. To not know in the perspective of faith is to remain humble and open to learning. When faith does not fill in the cracks in a crisis, then fear will. Therefore, faith is an attitude that we create where it is the acceptance of not knowing. Unknowing is what creates faith.

Practicing Creative Visualization to Encourage Self-Compassion

Creative visualization is a mental technique that harnesses our imagination to make our goals and dreams a reality. When used the right way, creative visualization has been proven to improve the lives of the people who have used it, and it also increases the success and prosperity rate of the individual. Creative visualization unleashes a power that can alter your social and living environment and circumstances, it causes beneficial events to happen, attracts positivity in work, life, relationships, and goals.

Creative visualization is not a magic potion. It uses the cognitive processes of our mind to purposely generate an array of visual mental imagery to create beneficial physiological, psychological or social effects such as increasing wealth, healing wounds to the body or alleviating psychological issues such as anxiety and sadness. This method uses the power of the mind to attract good energy and really, it is the magic potion behind every success.

Mostly, a person needs to visualize an individual event or situation or object or desire to attract it into their lives. This is a process that is similar to daydreaming. It only uses the natural process of the power of our mind to initiate positive thoughts and natural mental laws. Successful people like Oprah and Tiger Woods and Bill Gates use this technique, either consciously or unconsciously, attracting success and positive outcomes into their lives by visualizing their goals as already attained or accomplished.

- **The Power of Thoughts and Creative Visualization**

So how does this work and why is it so important to us?

Well, our mind is a powerful thing. With only the power of our mind, we can reach amazing success, or we can also spiral out of control. It swings both ways. Our subconscious mind accepts the ideals and thoughts that we often repeat, and when our mind accepts it, then your mindset also changes accordingly, and this influences your habits and actions. Again, a domino effect happens where you end up meeting new people or getting into situations or circumstances that lead you to your goal. Our thoughts come with a creative power that can mold our life and attract whatever we think about.

Remember the saying that goes 'mind over matter?' When we set our mind to do it, our body does what our mind tells us. Our thoughts travel from mind, body, and soul but believe it or not; it can travel from one mind to another because it is unconsciously picked up by the people you meet with every day and usually, most of the people you end up meeting are the ones who can help you achieve your goals.

You probably think and repeat certain thoughts everyday pretty often, and you probably do this consciously or unconsciously. You probably have focused your thoughts on your current situation or environment and subsequently, create and recreate the same events and circumstances regularly. While most of our lives are somewhat routine, we can always change these thoughts by visualizing different circumstances and situations, and in a way, create a different reality for you to focus on new goals and desires.

- **Changing Your Reality**

Honestly, though, you can change your 'reality by changing your thoughts and mental images. You aren't creating magic here; all you are doing is harnessing the natural powers and laws that inhibit each and every one of us. The thing that separates normal, average folk with wildly successful people is that the successful ones have mastered their thoughts and mental images while the rest of us are still learning or trying to cope. Changing your thoughts and attitude changes and reshapes your world.

Take for example you plan on moving into a larger apartment and instead of wallowing in self-pity such as the lack of money, do this instead- alter your thoughts and attitude and visualize yourself living in a larger apartment. It isn't difficult to do because it's exactly like daydreaming.

- **Overcoming Limited Thinking**

You may think daydreaming about positive things and money and success and great relationships are nothing but child's play but in fact, creative visualization can do wonders. Though that, it may be hard for different individuals to immediate alter their thoughts. Limits to this positive thinking are within us and not the power of our mind- we control it.

It might sound like its easy to change the way you think, but the truth is, it takes a lot of effort on your side to alter your thoughts at least in the immediate future. But never for a second doubt that you can't. Anything that you put your mind to work on, it can be done.

We often limit ourselves due to our beliefs and our thoughts and to the life we know. So the need to be open-minded is an integral part of positive thinking. The bigger we dare to think, the higher and great our changes, possibilities and opportunities. Limitations are created within our minds, and it is up to use to rise above all these obstacles.

Of course, it takes time to change the way we think and see things and broaden our horizons, but small demonstrations of changing our minds and the way we think will yield bigger results in due time.

- **Guidelines for Creating Visualization**

Concise Guidelines for Creative Visualization:

Step 1: Define your goal.

Step 2: Think, meditate and listen to your instinct, ensure that this is the goal you want to attain

Step 3: Ascertain that you only want good results from your visualization, for you and for others around you.

Step 4: Be alone at a place that you will not be disturbed. Be alone with your thoughts.

Step 5: Relax your body and your mind

Step 6: Rhythmically breathe deeply several

Step 7: Visualize your goal by giving it a clear and detailed mental image

Step 8: Add desire and feelings into this mental image- how you would feel etc

Step 9: Use all your five senses of sight, hearing, touch, taste and smell

Step 10: Visualize this at least twice a day for at least 10 minutes each time

Step 11: Keep visualizing this day after day with patience, hope and faith

Step 12: Always keep staying positive in your feelings, thoughts and words

Staying positive can be easy, it is all about training your mind. When you do feel doubts, and negative thoughts arise, replace them with positive thoughts. Also remember to keep an open mind because opportunities come in various ways so when you see it, you can take advantage of them. Every morning, or each time you conclude your visualization session, always end it with this 'Let everything happen in a favorable way for everyone and everything involved.'

Creative visualization will open doors but it takes time and whenever you feel you are in a position of advantage, take action. Do not be passive or wait for things to fall on your lap. Perhaps you've met someone who can put yours in a position of advantage to reach your goal or perhaps you've landed a job that has the possibility of enabling you to travel. All these things come into your life, and if you have an open mind, you can see the possibilities more vividly.

When you use the power of imagination for you and the people around you, always do it for good. Never try creative visualization to obtain something forcibly that belongs to others (like someone else's husband or wife or a managerial position someone else rightfully achieved but you want as well). Also, don't harm the environment.

Most visualized goals happen in a natural and gradual manner, but there can be times that can happen in a sudden and expected manner too. Be realistic with your goals, though. Don't visualize a unicorn and expect it to turn up. If money is what you desire, you know that it just will not drop from the sky. You may or may not win it in the lottery. But the chances or possibilities are higher when you go through life with a new job, or you get a promotion, or you end up making a business deal.

It is always better to think and visualize what you actually want because you do not want to attract situations that are negative, in your quest to fulfill your goals and desires.

Using Affirmations

Affirmations have helped many people make significant changes in their lives and the people around them. Do they work for everyone? Why do some people have achieved success using this technique but some people do not get anything from it?

- **What are Affirmations?**

Affirmations are positive and direct statements that help an individual overcome self-sabotaging and negative thoughts. It helps a person visualize and believe in their goals, dreams, and abilities. In other words, you are affirming to yourself and helping yourself make positive changes to your life goals. Affirmations have the power to work because it can program a person's mind into believing a concept. The mind is known not to know the difference between what is real or fantasy. That is why when you watch a movie; you tend to empathize with the characters on the screen even though you know it's just a movie. But as soon as you leave the cinema, you are back into reality but can't help feel sorry or happy for the characters.

There are both positive and negative affirmations and some of these affirmations such as being told you are smart when you were a child or being told that you are clumsy can stick with us in both our conscious or unconscious mind. When we face failure, we tend to over-calculate the risks we are taking and work out the worst possible scenario which is usually the emotional equivalent of our parents or guardian deserting us.

We imagine an entirely dreadful scenario in our minds that we convince ourselves that trying to change isn't a good thing at all. Thus, it makes us lose out on opportunities for success and then when we actually do fail (because our mind is already convinced we'll fail anyway) the whole experience of affirmation that we give ourselves is that we are not cut out for success, or it is not in our karma to succeed, and then, we settle.

If a negative belief is firmly rooted in our subconscious mind, then it will have the ability to override any positive affirmation even when we aren't aware of it.

This is one of the reasons why people do not believe in positive affirmations because it doesn't seem to be working. Their negative patterns are so high it just knocks out the sun!

So how do we add affirmations into our daily life and how can we make them prevail above our negative thinking? Here are some steps to follow:

Making Affirmations Work for You

Step 1- On a day that you are alone and not busy or distracted (if you don't have a time like this, then make one) list down all your negative qualities. Include any criticism that others have made of you and those that you have been holding onto. Remember that we all have flaws so do not judge. By acknowledging your mistakes, you can then move forward and work on your flaws, and you can make a shift in your life. When you write these down, take note to see if you are holding any grudges along the way or holding on to it. For example, do you feel tightness or dread in your heart?

Step 2- Begin to write out an affirmation on the positive aspect of your self-assessment. Use powerful statement words to beef up this assessment. Instead of saying 'I am worthy' say 'I am extremely cherished and remarkable.'

Step 3- Practice every day reading this affirmation loudly for five minutes at least three times a day in the morning, afternoon and at night before going to sleep. You can do this while shaving or putting your make up on, or when you are fixing yourself a cup of tea or if you are in the shower. At best, look in the mirror, so you look at yourself and repeat these positive statements. You can also write these affirmations in your notebook at any time you feel like it. Take note of how your writing changes over time. If we do not like something, often writing this down will encompass using smaller handwriting but if we right in big and bold letterings, we are increasing the affirmation of this. This is really a mindfulness journey to get to the agenda of positive affirmation.

Step 4- To enhance the impact, do body movements such as placing your hand on your heart when you felt uncomfortable writing out a negative criticism of yourself in Step 1. As you work on reprogramming your mind to alter it from the concept of affirmation to a real and definite personification of the quality that you see.

Step 5- Get someone to help you repeat your affirmations. This can be a friend or a gym coach or just about anyone that you feel safe with. For example, if they are saying that you are cherished and remarkable, and then connect this statement with your situations such as 'excellent colleague' or 'good fathering.' If you are not comfortable with doing this with someone, then look at your reflection in the mirror and reinforce your positive message.

Affirmations can be an incredibly powerful tool that can help you change your state of mind, alleviate your mood and more importantly, ingrain the changes your desire into your life. But for all of this to happen, you first need to identify the negative and the work on getting rid of them in your life.

Examples of Positive Affirmation

Here are some examples of positive affirmations that you can use to relate to the various areas of your development:

- I know, accept and am true to myself
- I believe in myself and have confidence in my decisions
- I eat a balanced diet, exercise regularly and get plenty of rest
- I always learn from my mistakes
- I know I am capable of anything and can accomplish anything I set my mind to
- I have flaws and I am not perfect but that's ok because I am human
- I never, ever give up

- I can adapt and accept what I have no control over
- I make the best of every situation
- I always look at the bright side of life
- I enjoy life to the fullest
- I stand up for what I believe in, my morals and my values
- I treat others with respect and recognize their individuality
- I can make a difference
- I can practice understanding, patience and compassions
- I am always up to learn new things and be open-minded
- I live in the moment and learn from my past and prepare for my future

These are just some of the positive affirmations that you can use to be optimistic and pursue a fulfilling and happy mindset. Have fun in creating your own affirmations or tailor the above to suit your needs and situation. Most of the affirmations above can be used daily to uplift, inspire and motivate you and those around you.

Mindfulness Meditation for Self-Compassion

Have you thought about meditation or have you done meditation before? Meditation does wonders to your body, mind and soul. When it comes to practising self-compassion, mindful meditation helps you incorporate this into your daily life more frequently. Keep in mind that mindful meditation isn't only helpful for self-compassion but it also helps us deal with the negativity that we face when we want to practice self-compassion.

Exercise 1 – Mindful Breathing

Breathing is an essential part of the meditative experience, so it is only natural that we should

exercise this too. Whenever you meditate, you're breathing mindfully when you focus on each purposeful breath that goes in and out of your body. Mindful breathing doesn't just have to happen when you're meditating, it can be done anywhere and at any time whether you're sitting, standing or just walking about. Make it a habit to breathe mindfully and you'll find it much easier to do so during your meditation sessions.

1. Start by bringing your attention and focus to your breathing.
2. Breathe in slowly for approximately 3 seconds, and then release that breathe slowly, counting to 3 seconds again.
3. During this exercise, you should focus and be thinking of nothing else except your breathing. Do not think about the tasks you need to do, or a meeting that is coming up at work. Think about nothing but your breathing in and out, counting the seconds as you do.
4. Concentrate on the air that is filling your lungs as you breathe in, the way it makes your body feel, and when you release your breathe, imagine all the stress and the tension leaving your body as you do.

You can do this for 1-2 minutes at a time throughout the day, several times a day and you're already on your way towards improving each meditation session when you get better at learning to control your breathing.

Exercise 2 – Awareness

When you meditate, you learn to become more aware of your body, your mind and your thoughts, aware of what is happening all around you when your eyes are closed because your other senses become heightened when your eyes are shut. Being mindfully aware helps you sharpen your focus and remain alert to not just your surroundings, but your thoughts as well. For example, if you were mindfully aware about your thoughts, you will have better control when it comes to keeping any negative thought or emotion at bay.

Exercising your awareness throughout the day will help sharpen your alertness towards everything around you. Not just around you, but within you too. Beginners often find focusing on awareness to be a struggle in the beginning, because its so easy to let our thoughts drift and get distracted by everything else. Training yourself to be more aware will help you better connect your mind and body during your meditation sessions, so it's a good idea to practice these throughout the day to help you sharpen your focus and cultivate a heightened sense of awareness.

1. Start by choosing an activity or an object to focus on. Pick something that you would normally do without thinking twice about it, like opening the door or getting dressed in the morning for example.
2. Once you've got your object or activity, start to really, actively pay attention to what you're doing. If you're opening the door, concentrate on it. Reach for the doorknob and be aware of how it feels in your hand, and the motion of pulling the door towards you or away from you. Stop and appreciate how lucky you are to be healthy and fit enough to walk out your front door with a destination and a purpose in mind.
3. When you're getting dressed in the morning, focus and be aware of what you're doing instead of just going through the motions. Concentrate on how the fabric of your clothes feel in your hand, and even stop to appreciate how fortunate you are to be able to have a selection of clothes to choose from as you go through your closet looking for something to wear.
4. Before you eat, be aware of the food that is in front of you, how good it smells, the shapes, the colors. As you take each bite and begin to chew, be aware of how the food tastes and you take each bite with purpose.

Eventually, being mindfully aware is something that will come much easier, and the more you practice the easier you will find it is to concentrate on what you're doing or thinking without becoming easily distracted by other thoughts around you.

Exercise 3 – Mental Focus

Successful meditation involves being able to concentrate and not let your thoughts get easily distracted, which means you're going to need to work on improving your focus. Exercises to improve your focus are simple enough, here's what you can do:

1. Pick an object to focus on and place it in front of you.
2. When you're ready, set a timer and start to focus on the object and nothing else.
3. Concentrate on that object and keep staring at it for as long as you can.
4. When your mind begins to wander, stop and make a note of how long you managed to concentrate on that object before your mind started to drift.
5. Next round, do the same thing but try to go for a longer time this time around, aiming to beat your previous record.

Gradually, you should be able to focus on the object in front of you for longer periods of time before you find yourself getting distracted. The longer you can focus on the object, the better your focusing abilities will become.

PART IV

Chapter 1: Self-Esteem and Valuing Yourself

Imagine waking up in the morning and being full of life. You are energetic as you get out of bed and are ready to attack the day because nothing can stop you. Any type of challenge that comes your way, you are prepared to face it head-on and overcome it. You take pride in your work and relationships because you understand their worth. You also understand the value that you bring to the day, so you carry yourself with strength and dignity.

On the other hand, picture yourself waking up in a crummy mood. You are not looking forward to the day ahead, and no matter what good things may come, they are quickly tossed aside, and your mind wanders towards the negative side. You suffer from anxiety throughout the day, and you avoid any challenging situation you can because you lack faith in yourself.

These two mindsets are entirely different from one another, but they are related to the same thing: Your self-esteem. Self-esteem is the amount of respect that you place on yourself. It is how much you value your skills and ability to handle life and all its circumstances. Those who place a high value on themselves have a high level of self-esteem. Those who set a low value on themselves suffer from low self-esteem.

Your self-esteem is also your self-worth, and you mustn't put a low price tag on your abilities.

Having high self-esteem does not mean you ignore your flaws. It means that you love yourself despite all of them. You recognize your weaknesses, and therefore, are more likely to fix them. In the end, you love yourself because of your own self-beliefs.

As we grow up, we are constantly surrounded by things that affect our psyche. Our ego is the part of our mind that has a direct relationship with the outside world. When we experience an event or interact with a specific individual, it will determine how we feel at that exact moment. If the situation is upsetting, then it can bring out a range of different emotions in us. For those who are dealing with low self-esteem, they will easily be triggered by an outside event. For example, if someone calls us a negative name, it might make us feel sad or angry. This one incident could ruin our whole day in an instant. If we are experiencing negativity over a long period of time, then these thoughts will slowly enter into our subconscious and unconscious mind, where they stay forever, unless we purposefully remove them.

If you have a healthy level of self-esteem, then these situations will roll off your back. Negative people or situations will not change the feelings you have towards yourself because you will be in complete control of your emotions. I am not suggesting that being insulted will not be hurtful for this type of individual, but they will understand how to manage it and not let it affect them negatively. They don't define themselves by other people's opinions.

I can talk all day about the extreme benefits of self-esteem, as there are many. The focus of this book, though, is how to develop and build your self-esteem, even if you have been suffering from low levels of it your whole life. I am working off the assumption that you are in the camp of low self-esteem. Therefore, you already know how it feels, because you are personally living it.

How Low Self-Esteem Is Developed

The first step in dealing with low self-esteem is recognizing that you have it. Now that we have established that, it is important to determine why you have low self-esteem.

The Different Types of Parents

One of the major contributing factors to our self-esteem is our parents and how they raised us. Our mother and father are generally the first people we become close to. How they interact with us will initially determine how we value ourselves. Even if a parent is loving, there are still specific tendencies that can be counterproductive to use raising our self-worth.

While parents often push their children to succeed, some can become overbearing to the point where they use ridicule, harsh criticisms, and even abuse to ensure their children stay on the straight path. While some parents do not have malicious intent when they become disapproving authority figures, others will purposefully look down on their kids and make them feel inferior. Children who grow up under these conditions grow into adults who are never comfortable in their own skin.

On the opposite end of the overbearing caregiver is the uninvolved caregiver who does not care one bit. They ignore their children as if they are not necessary. In fairness, this can often be done unintentionally. For example, the parents work so much and become excessively focused on their jobs. They are obsessed with making a living and ignore the people closest to them, including their children. When children get ignored by the influential adults in their lives, they become confused about their place in the world. They feel forgotten and unimportant, and therefore, they believe their existence to be bothersome to people.

Another parental issue that affects children is the parents or caregivers who are in constant conflict. When these adults fight and throw hurtful language at one another, especially in front of children, they absorb these negative emotions. These children can feel like they contributed to the fighting in some way. Growing into adulthood, these same children will feel like they are the cause of so many different conflicts, simply because they were nearby.

Bullying

Bullying has been an issue for children and adults alike for generations. The powerful always seem to push around the weak. With children, this power is usually in the form of physical dominance. The bigger and stronger child picks on the smaller and weaker one. Of course, the bullying can be mental or psychological, too, if the child can pull it off.

Bullying can also become a significant contributor to low self-esteem. A child who is constantly bullied in any way will develop a poor self-image about themselves. Unfortunately, bullying will never go away. What matters in these situations is the support that children receive from their parents. The way the adults in a child's life handle the aftermath of bullying will play a major role in their mindset development.

Many children do not have a comforting environment to come home to, which is detrimental to their psyche. After experiencing abuse outside the come, they walk through their front door and experience even more of it. This makes a child feel worthless and abandoned. They become lost further into the abyss and think they do not belong anywhere. Having unsupportive parents will magnify the effects of bullying.

Furthermore, some parents were over-supportive. These are the ones who coddled their children and gave them no coping skills to deal with the outside world. As a result, they will be ill-prepared to deal with the cruel world that exists out there, which is not going away anytime soon. When children become adults and enter the real world, they will face some harsh criticisms that will challenge their beliefs about who they are. If they were always buttered up as children, they would not understand how to face rejection, insults, or people being mean to them.

No parent wants their children to feel bad, but they cannot be shielded from disappointment their whole lives. Once they do face this disappointment in the real world, they will fall apart because they have no actual self-worth. All of their value is tied to the compliments that other people give them.

I know I have been singling out parents here, and that's because they are the adults a child spends the most amount of time with. However, other adults, like extended family members, teachers, coaches, or counselors, can also do their part in providing a supportive atmosphere for the children in their lives.

Trauma

Trauma can be physical, emotional, or sexual, and no matter what kind you were a victim of, it will devastate your self-esteem, especially as a child. With trauma, you are being forced into a position against your will, which makes you feel like you've lost power and control of your situation.

Situations like this will make you feel worthless. You will even blame yourself for causing the trauma or abuse. This is a method many people use to gain control back into their lives. They believe that by taking the blame, they will be able to manage the situation the next time it comes around

Children do not have control over who is in their lives. This means they are often stuck in abusive situations and have no way of getting out of it. If they are lucky, someone will recognize it, and they will help them get out.

A child who goes through trauma will grow into an adult who is unsure of themselves in many ways. They will never feel like they are good enough, will always feel like they are to blame for specific situations, and will have a distrust for humanity in general.

I know I have spoken about a lack of trust throughout this book. A significant part of having self-esteem is being able to put your faith into the unknown. When you lack trust, this faith does not exist, and therefore, you will always be paranoid and never fully confident in any situation.

Now, think back on your life and determine the traumatic events you may have gone through. How did these affect your psyche at that moment? How you felt on the inside when these various circumstances occurred will help you understand if they contributed to a lack of self-esteem.

We went over these issues simply to help you recognize the underlying causes of the value you place on yourself. There is nothing we can do about these situations now, but we can learn from them and work on ways to overcome our mental blocks to positive self-esteem.

The Science of Self-Esteem

There has been a lot of research done on the genetic components of low self-esteem. While people can be born with certain levels of chemicals that influence their emotions and brain activity, there is no conclusive evidence that people are born with high or low self-esteem. Even twins who grew up in different environments were found to have different qualities related to their self-worth, even though various other personality traits were similar. As of now, environmental factors seem to play a much more significant role.

Of course, this does not mean that there is no scientific component to all of this. As we go through various life stages, our brain development occurs based on life experiences. The actions we take and the thoughts we create make numerous neural pathways in our brain and nervous system, which determine our future behavior. For example, if we continuously have negative feelings, our mind becomes wired in a certain way to produce these same thoughts in the future. As a result, you habitually think negatively in every situation you come across.

Now that we have established what low self-esteem is, our goal in the next chapter is to help you rewire your brain, so you can start living with high self-esteem.

Chapter 2: How You Can Matter to Yourself

"Confront the dark parts of yourself, and work to banish them with illumination and forgiveness. Your willingness to wrestle with your demons will cause your angels to sing."

-August Summer

Now that we know what self-esteem is, it is hard to deny the role it plays in our lives. Any type of pursuit, whether personal, professional, relationships, or health, will require you to place a high value on yourself; otherwise, you will never progress forward as you should. At this moment, I want you to recognize the past mistakes that brought you to where you are now, but also forgive yourself for them because you can do nothing to change the past. You can learn from it, though, and build a new future where you actually value yourself and the gifts you bring to the world.

In the previous chapter, we discussed the numerous causes of low self-esteem, many of which stem from our childhood. Since our mindset took a long time to develop, it will take extreme effort with several actionable steps to change and overcome this thought-process. We will now discuss some specific steps and practices over the next few chapters you can engage in to improve your mindset and build-up your self-esteem.

We will approach this subject from many different aspects, so they can be combined to improve how you habitually think about yourself. Think of your mind as a structure that is built to think a specific way. Now imagine having to rebuild many different parts of that structure to change your thoughts. This is what we will be doing with all of the action steps we will go over.

How to Build Self-Awareness

Self-awareness means having the ability to understand the way you think, feel, and behave. This is a necessary quality to have if you want to fix your self-esteem. It is the best way to recognize if your actions correlate with low self-esteem. Once you become self-aware, you will know yourself much better. The following are some significant strategies you can employ right away.

Recognize What Bothers You About Other People

What bothers us most about other people are often the same qualities that we possess. For example, if someone is naturally aggressive, we may dislike it; however, it is a trait that we have, as well. We all have aspects of our personality that are unflattering, and since we don't want to admit them, we will ignore them fully. Ignorance is not bliss in the long-run, and if we do not pay attention to our negative qualities, they will rear their ugly heads at the most inopportune time. The next time a person is bothering you, stop and ask yourself if they are displaying something that is a reflection of you. Do you recognize their personality when you look in the mirror?

Meditate on Your Mind

Mindful meditation is a great way to learn about your thoughts and how they work. One of the main reasons we lack self-awareness is because we are thinking so much that our thoughts completely take over. Proper meditation allows us to separate ourselves from these thoughts and recognize that they do not fully encompass who we are. Through mindful meditation practices, you have the ability to observe your thoughts without becoming attached to them. Therefore, it is easier to see which ones deserve our attention and which ones do not. The following are some simple steps to get you started on this practice.

- Get comfortable by finding a quiet place that is as free from distractions as possible.
- Sit up with your back straight and chest out. It does not matter if you are in a chair or sitting cross-legged on the floor. You may even lie down flat on the floor.
- Take in some deep breaths through your nose and then out slowly through your mouth or nose. You should be able to feel the breaths down into your abdomen. This will help you relax.
- Pay attention to the sounds of your breaths and their rhythmic patterns. When you inhale, imagine breathing in joy and peace. When you breathe out, imagine getting rid of the toxicity in your mind.
- When you notice your thoughts wandering away from your breaths, immediately focus them back to the center. Take in your

- immediate surroundings and be in your present state. Do not think of the past or worry about the future.
- Make this practice a habit and do it routinely. Some of the best practitioners of mindful meditation have been doing it for years, and are still learning better ways to improve. These are all great steps to get you started and reorganize your mind.

As a side note, meditation is not only useful for self-awareness. It can help with stress and anxiety, communication, better sleep, improved focus on your goals, and overall mental health. All of this will lead back to higher self-esteem. Start off with five minutes and then build yourself up to 20-30. You will be amazed at how much clarity you will have about yourself.

Draw a Timeline of Your Life

Sit down with a notepad and try to remember as much as you can from the time of birth to where you are now. Pay special attention to significant moments that had a big impact on your life and circumstances, whether positive or negative. This practice will allow you to see certain moments of your life in context, which will give you a better idea of who you are. You will realize a lot about yourself and gain much self-awareness.

Identify Your Emotional Kryptonite

Think about the emotions that you absolutely hate having and try to avoid. For example, some individuals hate feeling sad so much that they drown this emotion with alcohol. The problem is, negative emotions are a gateway into our souls. They are trying to tell us something in a discrete way. If we pay attention to them as they are happening, we will learn a lot about our situation. If you are sad often, pay attention to why so you can finally address it.

Travel and Get Out a Little Bit

We often become stuck in our own little box and forget that there is a big world out there. Micro-travel, which means traveling to new destinations that are local to us, is a great way to get you out of your comfort zone and try out a new routine. Take frequent short trips if you can, and even travel abroad if this is feasible. This will help you gain a lot of awareness for the world around you, as well as teach you a lot about yourself. Travel to new destinations, even nearby, will significantly raise our self-awareness.

Pick Up a New Skill

Just like with travel, learning a new skill will force us to think and act in new ways, thereby forcing us to increase our self-awareness. We all develop certain routines as we grow older, and it causes us to go into a comfort zone. The main problem here is that it creates a strong, narrow-mindedness. Being willing to start something as a beginner will cultivate a level of flexibility in our minds and thoughts. The new skill does not have to be related to your career. It can also be hobbies like playing the piano, sculpting, or dancing.

Clarify Your True Values

How often do you sit down and assess what your true values are? If you are like most people, probably very seldomly. We often get so caught up in daily life that we have very little time for self-reflection, especially on the important things in life. As a result, we end up chasing false goals and not living the type of life we want to. People become so worried about moving up the career ladder and buying the latest fancy car, that they forget what actually makes them happy. In your case, you may have followed a safe career path rather than focus on what your true calling was.

A great technique you can perform is to set aside some time on a weekly or monthly basis and think about your life and circumstances. Ask yourself why you think you are here and what your purpose in life is? Also, imagine what a fulfilling life would look like for you. Spend about 30 minutes every time you do this. A major part of self-awareness is recognizing what really matters to you. This practice will be a great way to come to this understanding.

We tend to get lost in the monotony of life. So, it is important to practice these self-awareness techniques on a regular basis. Taking notice of your thoughts, behaviors, and actions in real-time is a special skill to have. It will go a long way in helping you build your self-esteem.

Chapter 3: Creating a Stronger Self

Going along the path of improved self-esteem, I will now discuss various strategies to strengthen your psyche. High self-esteem requires a strong mindset.

Managing Your Ego

I spoke briefly in chapter one about the ego. Our ego is basically our mind's direct connection to the outside world. What our environment gives, our ego responds. This means that whatever activities are going on around will make you feel a certain way, and this is directly the result based on how our ego responds. For example, if someone outshines us in some way, our ego will respond by making us feel inferior.

People who are not careful will have this aspect of the mind completely control them. As a result, the values they place on themselves are based on what the world thinks of them, rather than what they think of themselves. Every one of us has an ego to a certain degree, but the key is to not let it control us. We must learn to manage it properly so that our self-worth comes from within, rather than from what we can't control. The following are specific steps you can take to begin managing your ego so that it doesn't control you.

Don't Take Things Personally

Taking things too personally or literally can make you overthink and cause your mind to become infected. It's important to be at peace with yourself and realize that people do not always mean what they say. They are often angry or suffering from some other negative emotion. Even if they do mean it, people who treat others poorly have a problem within themselves, and not necessarily other people. In a moment where you are facing harsh words or actions, imagine your spot being replaced by someone else and watching the same people act in the same manner because, in most cases, they would. A big part of self-esteem is not caring what others think. This is a major step in that direction.

Accepts All of Your Mistakes

Accepting your mistakes, no matter how big or small is a positive way to work on your ego problems. Everyone makes mistakes, so there is no use in hiding them. Once you admit them, apologize, and move on, they no longer have control over you as you've released them from your psyche. Genuinely apologizing to someone is a great way to put your ego in check and grow as a person.

Stop Being Self-Conscious

Our ego prevents us from looking silly or goofy. We are so afraid of what others are thinking that we never let out guard down. This is a real definition of living in fear. If you have been acting this way for a while, then it's time to stop putting up a shield, and just let your silly self come out. You will actually be happier in the long run because showcasing your true self will attract your real friends. To stop being so self-conscious, try using the following steps.

- Shrug away your negative thoughts. This does not mean you should ignore them. Acknowledge that they are there, but then do not agree with them in any way.

- Don't put other people on pedestals. We have a tendency to do this, especially to those who we admire. Realize that they are regular people and not someone to bow down to.

- Think of a moment where you were self-conscious, and then imagine replacing yourself with someone you cared about in the position. If they felt the same way you did, then what would you tell them. Now, tell that same thing to yourself. We are often bigger critics of ourselves than we are other people.

- Accept yourself, with your faults and all. Remember that nobody is perfect, and if you want to gain a high level of self-esteem, then you must learn to love yourself, including your flaws.

- People are not paying as much attention to you as you may think. Part of our ego tells us that people are watching us and critiquing our every move. Understand that people are in their own world much of the time, and too busy in their personal self-doubts to pay attention to anyone else. Believe it or not, you are not the focus of attention all the time.

- Go do the thing that makes you self-conscious or nervous. Face it head-on, and you will realize it's not as bad as you may think. Do not let your awkwardness keep you on the sidelines. Jump in with both feet and dare to look foolish. If you hate dancing in front of people, join a dance class and do it several times a week. If you suck at basketball, go to the part and shoot hoops in front of people.

Realize That Your Ego Will Never Go Away

Controlling and managing your ego will have to become a routine in your life. It will never fully go away and will rear its ugly head at the most inopportune times if you let your guard down. Always be on high alert of your ego trying to take over, and you will continue to overcome it.

You Are Not the Best

I am not trying to be insulting here, but knowing that you are not going to be the best in every situation means that you understand your limitations. Everyone has limitations, so there is no sense in feeling bad over them. Accept that you are not perfect, but recognize that it does mean you cannot accomplish your goals. You may just need to work harder and focus more on certain areas.

Imagine Your Ego as Another Person

This step may seem ridiculous, but imagine your ego as another person. It is best to picture someone that you may listen, but never actually take advice from, like a whining child. Now, once you imagine your ego in this manner, allow it to speak and say what it needs, acknowledge it with a "thank you," and then move on. When you can actually picture your ego in this way, it will do a lot in stopping you from making significant mistakes.

Stop Bragging

There is no need to brag about your accomplishments. If they are great enough, other people will do the talking for you. The less you talk about yourself, the more humble you become, and humility is a major aspect of self-esteem. You never feel the need to talk yourself up.

Be Grateful for the Little Things

Gratitude is great for improving your attitude. When you start being grateful for the little things, you do not worry so much about the big things. Also, remember that some people cannot have what you have, no matter how hard they try. With the same token, some people will be in a different position than you, that you are unable to reach. That is okay. Just focus on yourself and what you have.

Learn to Compliment Others

People with large egos have a hard time admitting when others have done a great job. They feel it will take the spotlight off of them. Practicing paying even the smallest compliments to other people can help you take the attention off of your ego problems.

On top of these practices, we have gone over, a few other ways to get rid of your ego include:

- Embrace a beginner's attitude. Try something new regularly that forces you to challenge yourself. This will help you realize that you are not perfect at everything.
- Concentrate on the effort you put in, and not the results. You will be forced to see how much you put into an activity, and determine if you did too much, or not enough.
- Never stop learning, even if it's not something you will ever use. It keeps you humble.
- Validate yourself once in a while.
- Never expect rewards or recognition. Do what is right, simply because it is the right thing to do.
- Do not try to control everything.

Forgiving People

Since so much of our self-esteem is tied up in what the people of our past did or did not do for us, it is important to forgive those who may have harmed us. We often hold onto grudges, and this prevents us from moving forward. Part of having self-esteem is no longer allowing others to control us. If the actions of people in the past still impact the opinion we have of ourselves, then we are still under there control. The main idea of forgiveness is that you have the ability to move on without having to carry a heavy burden any longer. Here is what forgiveness does not mean:

- Condoning harmful behavior.
- Accepting someone back into your life.
- Forgetting the incident or incidents that harmed you.
- Having to talk to the person again in any way.
- You are helping the other person. Of course, this may be a secondary benefit, which is fine.

By forgiving someone, you are accepting the reality that they did something terrible to you, but it no longer has to define you. Forgiveness is 100 percent for your own benefit.

The first step in forgiveness is the willingness to actually forgive someone. Just imagine that the anger you have for someone is a bag of rocks that you have been carrying on your back. After many years, this becomes very exhausting, both physically and mentally. Now, imagine that forgiveness means dropping that bag of rocks forever. You will feel much better when you put down the bag, and you will feel much better once you forgive. When you are ready, then utilize the following steps to help you get past, well, your past.

- Think about the particular incidents that angered you. Accept that they happened and what your feelings were when they did. In order to forgive, you must acknowledge what happened. You cannot just ignore it. This is why forgetting is not part of the process. For example, the incident could have been that your parents were absent and did not pay any attention to you.

- Acknowledge the growth in yourself that happened after the incident occurred. What did it make you learn about yourself and the world? For example, if your parents were absent for much of your life, perhaps it taught you how to be independent and survive on your own. That is a pretty big deal.

- Now think about the other person. The one that actually caused the incident. Realize that they were working from a limited frame of mind and did not have the benefit of hindsight. When they harmed you in some way, they were probably trying to have one of their needs met. Think about what that need may have been, and if it changes your perspective on them. In reference to your parents, maybe they were absent and did not pay attention to you because they were worried about always having food on the table and a roof over your head. This caused them to work incessantly, and when they were home, they were too tired to give you the right amount of attention. It's possible that they hated being absent just as much as you did.

- Finally, say the words, "I forgive you." It is up to you whether you want to tell the person or not. In any event, tell yourself.

Forgiveness will help you put closure on your past so that you can focus on moving forward. This is an important step forward to gaining self-esteem. You will no longer be bound by what happened to you in the past; therefore, you will be free.

Overcoming Trauma

Since trauma plays a major role in a person's self-image, it is important to identify the negative thoughts that will lead to low self-esteem. Once you catch these thoughts, then you can combat them head-on. You may never forget about the trauma, but just like the hurt you received from people of your past, you can keep it from controlling you. The following are a few simple steps you can take to help you improve your negative self-image related to trauma. These practices have been used widely with people suffering from Post Traumatic Stress Disorder.

- Identify your negative thoughts. Once negative thoughts become part of your routine, they can easily slip by without getting caught. Self-monitoring can be a great way of increasing awareness of your thoughts and how they are affecting your mood and behavior. You must do this consciously. You may also sit down at the end of each day and run down what you did. Think about all of the negative thoughts you had, what caused them, and how you reacted. This can also make you more aware of them in the future. We often have specific triggers that affect our mood.

- Once you learn to identify negative thoughts, slow them down. The more you think about negative thoughts, the more intense they become. Therefore, once you identify them, distract yourself by thinking of something else. This is not about avoidance, but taking a step back and reducing the intensity of these thoughts. Often times, we cannot deal with negativity because it becomes so overwhelming. Once we remove ourselves from the situation a little bit, then we can manage things more appropriately.

- After reducing the intensity of your thoughts, it is now time to challenge them. Many times, we accept our thoughts at face value without actually questioning them. As a result, we do not actually know why we are thinking negatively during a certain situation. We just know that we always have. Challenge your thoughts by asking some of the following questions:

    o What evidence is there for having these thoughts?
    o What evidence is there that are against these thoughts?
    o Are there moments when these thoughts have not been true?
    o Do I only have these thoughts when I am sad, angry, or depressed, or do I have them when I am feeling okay, as well?
    o What advice would I give someone else who is also having these thoughts?
    o Is there any type of alternate explanation?

- Counter your negative thoughts further by using positive self-supportive statements. For example, you can tell yourself all of your recent accomplishments, the good qualities you do possess, or positive things you are looking forward to in the future, like starting a new job or taking a vacation. Basically, counter negative thoughts with positive ones. It is beneficial to write some of these down so you can refer to them in the future. When you are drowning in negativity, it can be difficult to come up with positive statements about yourself.

- As a side note, you do not have to use positive self-supportive statements exclusively when you are upset. You can tell them to yourself any time to build up your positivity.

Chapter 4: Changing Our Minds

For the final chapter in this section, we can start focusing on shifting the mindset fully towards high self-esteem. Once this occurs, we must continue to follow the strategies I have gone over to never lose your self-esteem. If you let your guard down, it will happen.

How To Ignore Things

Our self-esteem continues to remain low throughout our lives because we always let things bother us. Many of these things are beyond our control, so we should not pay them any mind. The reason people achieve their lifelong goals is that they don't let their surroundings affect their minds. The following are some ways to ignore what bothers you, so you can keep moving forward while loving yourself.

Stop Comparing Yourself To Others

The bottom line is, you are not someone else, and they are not you. Just because someone else looks great in a dress or suit, does not mean you have to, as well. Also, understand that other people will not look as good as you in certain outfits. Some people will look great all dressed up, while others pull off the casual look better.

If you are not comfortable, then you will never feel right in any situation.

Therefore, do not force yourself into something, simply because other people are doing it. Understand yourself through self-awareness and focus on the things that make you feel good. You can't compare yourself to others, and they can't compare themselves to you. Work on impressing the person in the mirror and no one else.

Ignore Societal Pressure

Have you ever done something because someone you don't like or even know might become impressed, even though they don't actually care about you? If this statement sounds ridiculous, imagine actually living. Oh, wait! Many people are already. This is because they are under some sort of societal pressure to live a certain way, even though most people in society don't matter to them in the long run. To stop allowing this to happen, ask yourself the following questions.

- Who will be responsible after I kill my dreams to produce a fake image, society, or me?
- Are the people around me genuinely concerned about my happiness? If not, then why do I care so much?
- Will the people pressuring me even matter five years from now?
- Am I alone in feeling this societal pressure?

After answering all of these questions, you will realize that your situation is not unique. Many people are pressured by society and trying to hold up a fake image. This means they are not happy because they are not willing to share their true selves. Ultimately, you will be living your own existence, whether you choose it or someone else does.

Start Living In The Present Moment

So many people live in the past, and therefore, their old mistakes still have an impact on their present state of mind. It's time to get over your past. The following are some tips to help you do so.

- Create some physical distance between yourself and the person or situation that is reminding you of your past. This could mean cutting off some close people or physically moving somewhere else.
- Stay busy working and improving yourself, that you have no time to worry about what happened in the past.
- Treat yourself like you would a best friend. We tend to be gentler with others than ourselves.
- Don't shut out negative emotions. Let them flow through you so you can overcome them.
- Don't expect an apology from other people. Even if you were wronged by them, they might not think so. Therefore, move on and accept that they haven't come to terms with anything, but you have.
- Give yourself permission to talk about your pain, even if it's just to yourself. In any event, let it out. Let the past pain escape out of you.

Leverage Your Purpose

This will give your life more meaning. First, leverage your purpose to serve others. Help someone else realize their dreams through your own unique talents. There are many unique ways to do this, including teaching, coaching, and mentoring. Do this on a volunteer basis. Whatever gives purpose to your life, share it with someone else.

Try out these different practices and feel yourself start ignoring all of the noise around you. It is distracting, and you must be able to filter it.

The Mindset Shift

We have gone over many different aspects of the mind and how to change certain thought-processes. What happens with these techniques is a total mindset shift. Instead of your mind being wired to think negatively about everything, including yourself, you will now habitually think in a positive way and understand the values you bring to the world, which are a lot. The goal of all of the previous practices and strategies is to rewire your neural pathways to help change your mindset.

Your mindset was developed over a long period of time, which means the neural pathways you have are build up pretty strong. For this reason, they must be worked on regularly to help break them down and build new ones up. So, do not treat these techniques as a one-and-done cure. They must become a regular part of your lifestyle. Once they are, then you will be amazed at the results you have. When your self-esteem is high, you will:

- Have no problem being yourself.
- Be able to disagree without attacking someone.
- Not be swayed so easily by the opinions of others.
- Be able to articulate your views and be able to defend them appropriately when challenged.
- No longer fear uncertainty.
- Be much more resilient and tough.
- Never need approval from anyone to live your life as you choose.
- Value yourself and have high self-worth, despite what others may think of you.
- Not act like you know everything.
- Be okay with not being perfect.
- Never again let your past define who you are.

Once you go from low to high self-esteem, you will feel like a completely different person. You will still acknowledge your past pain, but it will not control you.

Now That Your Self-Esteem is High

After going through all of the practices, thoughts, and feelings inside of you will be different because you will have effectively restructured your mind. The plan now is to keep revisiting these techniques, so you never fall back into the abyss ever again. Now that your self-esteem is high, you will sense the following beliefs flowing through you.

- No matter what you've done, you are worthy of love. You understand your past mistakes, but will not degrade yourself over them.
- You are not defined by your "stuff." You will enjoy what you have, but your happiness will not be dependent on it.
- You will allow yourself to feel all of your emotions, and not be ashamed of them.
- You won't care if you miss out on things. You will feel okay about staying alone because your company is good enough.
- You will not be worried about what happens to you, because you will be able to respond appropriately, There will be challenges, but the end result will be in your favor.
- You will be doing what you love. You will look forward to every day.
- You will understand that people are judging you based on something within themselves.
- You will never think the world revolves around you. There is a higher power out there greater than anything that exists on Earth. This does not have to be a diety, but it certainly can be for you.
- You will find things to be grateful for every day. Because you are looking, you will find them.

PART V

Chapter 1: Why So Sensitive?

"For a highly sensitive person, a drizzle feels like a monsoon."

-Anonymous

When something out of the ordinary happens, and it is relatively minor, you may become a little surprised, sad, anxious, or happy, depending on what the situation is. Even though the event happened out of nowhere, it elicits a minor emotional response. This will be the case if your emotional reactions are that of a normal individual. However, if you are part of the subset of the population which is highly sensitive, then your response will be anything but minor.

Imagine going completely over the top with your feelings when something out of the ordinary happens in your life. If you go through a distraught situation, you become much more saddened than those around you. If a friend has something good happen to them, you will act more excited than they do. When someone is loud, you feel it to your core. If this sounds like you, then you might be a highly sensitive person.

Individuals who are highly sensitive display stronger reactivity to external and internal stimuli, whether emotional, physical, or social. They are thought to have deeper sensitivities at the central nervous system. It is estimated that about 15-20 percent of the population falls under this umbrella. Highly sensitive persons are believed to be much more disturbed by violence or tension. If they see something bad happen on the news, they will be distraught and might even be bothered by it the whole day. In contrast, someone who is not in their shoes will just think about it for a moment. On the flip side, if you make them happy, they will be exceptionally excited beyond control. It's how they are built.

This may not sound like a big deal to most. You have probably known several people who are overly emotional. However, this goes beyond just crying a little extra during a movie. If you were to go inside the mind of a highly sensitive person, what you are likely to experience would overwhelm you instantly. If you are living with this mindset, then you know exactly what I am talking about.

Despite what people may think, highly sensitive people are not dramatic for no reason. They often cannot help the way they react in certain situations. At least, not without becoming aware of it first. These individuals will often notice things much more acutely than other people do. This relates especially to the feelings of others. While most individuals will simply overlook the pain and suffering of someone else, a highly sensitive person will be more aware of their emotions. They may not know exactly what is wrong, but just that something is okay. They will pick up on the subtleties of body language, facial expressions, and tone of voice. Even if they don't know an individual, they will be in-tune with the vibes the person puts off. All sensitivity radars will be off the charts.

How To Tell If You're In The Camp

If you have always felt a little different than everybody else around you, then you might be dealing with a highly sensitive personality. Of course, there are many different attributes to consider before knowing for sure. The following are some of the signs of being in this camp. Once you understand whether you're a highly sensitive person or not, then we can proceed forward.

- You are extremely unsettled by cruelty or violence. While most people don't enjoy violence, a highly sensitive person will become extremely disturbed or physically ill by it, even if they don't see it personally.
- You are frequently emotionally exhausted because of how others feel. Essentially, other people and their feelings have a deep impact on you.
- Time crunches make you extremely anxious and overwhelmed. While approaching deadlines can make anyone's hair get raised, it is exponentially greater for a highly sensitive person.
- You enjoy going int solitude at the end of the day to reduce your stimulation levels.
- You are very jumpy and become frightened quickly.
- You are a very deep thinker. You often reflect on your life and experiences to process everything. You will also play events in your head over and over again.
- You seek to find answers to life's questions and wonder why things are the way they are.
- You are startled easily by sudden, loud noises.
- You have reduced pain tolerance.
- You have a rich inner world. You probably grew up with many imaginary friends and might still have them as an adult. You frequently go into a fantasy world.
- You are extremely upset by change, whether positive or negative. It can really throw you off.

- You are very sensitive to the environmental stimuli around you, like the birds chirping, sirens, new smells, or unusual sites. This is because all of your senses are heightened.
- When you're hungry, you become angry too.
- You hate conflict and disagreements. You want people to get along and not fight with each other. You definitely avoid confrontation if you can.
- You are very thin-skinned. You do not take criticism well, whether it is constructive or not.
- You're very conscientious of making mistakes. You're not perfect, but you try extremely hard to be.
- The beauty of your surroundings moves you deeply. Whether it is artwork, a rich scent, or a delicious looking meal, you are enthralled by all of it.
- You will compare yourself to others and often feel inferior as a result.
- You are very perceptive and insightful. You pick up on things that others don't.

If you have been dealing with the issue of being highly sensitive, then you have probably been looked down upon your whole life. People may have told you to toughen up, be less sensitive, or grow a backbone. Don't take any of these statements personally because these individuals did not know better. In fact, you may not have known better and thought there was something wrong with you. Well, as you read further, you will actually begin to understand your unique gifts.

What Makes People Overly Sensitive?

There are many factors to consider when deciding on why you are a highly sensitive person. If having these feelings is an anomaly for you, meaning it's not your normal personality, then it is probably a unique life event that is causing you to behave in this manner. For example, losing a loved one, having poor health, not eating properly, or getting a lack of sleep may contribute to feelings of over sensitivity. However, if you have always been this way, then it goes well-beyond life events. It is ingrained in you to be a highly sensitive person.

Children who were severely criticized, bullied, or went through some type of abuse or trauma can also end up being highly sensitive. Their psyches took a major hit while they were children, so they grew up to be unsure of themselves, which may have contributed to their over-sensitivity, as a result.

Your highly sensitive feelings are likely to have a genetic component to them. So, you might have been born this way as it was passed on through your genes. Also, environmental and social factors may be involved. If your parents, or those you grew up around, were highly sensitive people, then you might have picked up on their personality traits and acquired them as your own. Of course, you can also end up completely opposite from your parents and other influential people, so their attributes may not mean anything in relation to you.

Overall, a highly sensitive person is thought to have a brain that is wired differently, so it has a lower threshold for the environment. So, any type of stimulus will have an exponential effect on them. Many of these characteristics can be seen in babies, as some infants are much more emotional and sensitive to things like sound. This further suggests that people are born highly sensitive, rather than made. In the mid-1990s, husband and wife psychology duo, Arthur and Elaine Aron, coined the term "sensory-processing sensitivity," which is the official scientific phrase used to describe a highly sensitive person. Through their research, the husband and wife duo stated further that the nervous system of someone with sensory-processing sensitivity had variations in their nervous system that was different from others who did not display highly sensitive qualities.

Negative Aspects Of Being A Highly Sensitive Person

Being in the camp of high sensitivity can certainly have their advantages, which we will go over in the next chapter. For now, I will discuss the negative aspects of being a highly sensitive person. This personality trait can impact every area of your life, and if you are not careful, it can create a lot of pain and suffering in the long run. Unfortunately, people will take advantage of the kind qualities of a sensitive individual, and the results are not always pleasant.

In The Workplace

If you are like the majority of people in the world, then you probably spend much of your time in the workplace. Here, you will have regular interactions with your coworkers and those in upper management. While certain things in the workplace may be a slight struggle or annoyance for most individuals, a highly sensitive person may have their whole workflow and mood affected in a significant way. The following are certain obstacles that only a highly sensitive person would understand and contend within the workplace.

- A strong aroma in the office can completely throw off a highly sensitive person. These can be smells that come from different foods or from someone wearing a lot of perfume.

- Other sensory issues like bright colors or loud sounds in the workspace, can severely affect their focus and ability to do their job.
- Trying to complete last-minute deadlines without proper planning can cause a highly sensitive person to become overwhelmed quickly. This is definitely not when they do their best work.
- Criticism from a boss or employee can truly mess with a highly sensitive person's head. They may even react in an unorthodox fashion, like having a mental breakdown, crying excessively, or running out of the office. They often cannot help it as it is an instantaneous reaction.
- Highly sensitive people will have a hard time speaking up and asking for what they want or need. They hate rocking the boat and definitely don't want to upset anyone else. As a result, they are often overlooked for many opportunities.
- These individuals are often seen as weak and ineffectual, so people will walk all over them. The highly sensitive person will usually let them.
- They are usually overstressed, even if it's a normal workday with nothing unusual going on. Anything in their environment can make them feel this way. Remember that highly sensitive people are more prone to be affected by environmental stimuli.
- There will be constant comparison with coworkers, and the highly sensitive person will always feel like they come up short.
- Wearing professional clothes, like ties, high-heels, or various other things that are uncomfortable, are highly bothersome to you.

As a highly sensitive person, you must be aware of these unique traits and how they will make you react. Otherwise, your experience at work will become constant suffrage.

In Their Personal Lives

Highly sensitive people will also deal with others in their personal lives, both at home and in various relationships. Their personality traits will often not do them any favors in this aspect of their lives, either. As a highly sensitive person, you will have extremely emotional and sometimes hostile relationships with those close to you. The following are some issues you may run into.

- Highly sensitive people will sense when their friends and family are going through some issues. They will also allow these emotions to overwhelm them.
- If a highly sensitive person gets asked to do something, in most cases, they will say yes, no matter how busy their schedule is or what they have planned. Saying no is a true challenge.
- These individuals are their own worst critic and will be excessively hard on themselves for something, while easily forgiving someone else for the same issues.
- They are often poor with self-care because they are too busy worrying about others.
- They are more sensitive to trouble and conflict within a relationship. They will become stressed easily during a conflict.
- They will have a lot of self-doubt about their abilities, which will show in their personal relationships. They will usually be the ones to submit and compromise full.
- They will have a hard time asking their friends for anything.
- It will be very easy to hurt a highly sensitive person's feelings. Plus, they can be manipulated easily.

As you can see, a highly sensitive person will not have an easy time with their personal relationships. They will usually be the givers and never the takers. These qualities can wear down on them and create much emotional and psychological harm if not dealt with accordingly.

Now that we have a picture of what a highly sensitive person is, you probably have a pretty good idea if you are one or not. We will get into more detail about the positive qualities of this personality trait.

Chapter 2: Embrace Your Sensitivities

I know I was pretty hard on highly sensitive people in chapter one and did not paint them in the most positive light. It is hard to imagine that these individuals actually have positive qualities. However, just because a highly sensitive person has flaws and weaknesses does not mean they don't have significant strengths too. In this section, I will go over the reasons why being a highly sensitive person is a good thing and how people can start embracing this aspect of themselves.

Benefits Of Being a Highly Sensitive Person

There are actually many great qualities to being a highly sensitive person, and the world is lucky to have individuals like this. Sensitivity is falsely depicted as being undesirable, which you have probably noticed in your own life. I am here to tell you that it is not a negative trait to have. With all of the controversy surrounding it, the benefits are often overlooked. But, they cannot be ignored any longer.

Having A Depth Of Experience And Feelings

Experiencing the world with heightened emotions gives you a deeper meaning in everything around you. You learn to find joy in the smallest things, which means you have the ability to find good in every area of life. You learn to experience life in a totally different way as a highly sensitive person and notice beauty in the subtleties of life.

Self-Awareness

Self-awareness means having a strong sense of who you are and where you belong in the world. A highly sensitive person has a keen self-awareness. They are hyper tuned in to their emotions, and the reactions that follow them. While a highly sensitive person understands their high levels of emotional volatility, they eventually realize that other people do not process feelings in the same manner that they do. What throws their minds for a loop, will barely be a blip on the radar for someone else.

Intuitive Nurturing Skills

The highly sensitive person is naturally good at nurturing others. Because of their ability to feel deeply, they have a strong desire to bring happiness to other people. They have the instinct to care for others and will support them, so they feel loved and appreciated.

A Knack For Forming Close relationships

Highly sensitive people may take a while to open up to somebody, but once they do, they form strong bonds in the process. They will become the best companions a person can have. The reason highly sensitive people are choosy with making friends is because they can feel the energy of others around them. If the energies don't mesh, they know the relationships won't be a good fit.

Highly sensitive people are not interested in casual acquaintances, but in developing meaningful relationships. They want to be around individuals who make them feel comfortable.

Appreciating The Small Things In Life

Highly sensitive people are also highly sensitive to things that bring them joy. This means they can find joy in even the smallest things in life. If they are having a bad day, hearing a good song on the radio can completely change their mood.

Why Highly Sensitive People Make Great Friends

As we move through life, we meet and develop relationships with many different people. While we get along and also get to know these individuals well, how many of them truly become great friends? It is rare to find friends who understand us for who we are, leave us feeling warm and make us believe that we are important. A highly sensitive person is a friend who has all of these abilities. These individuals become the best kinds of friends because of the attributes they possess. The following are a few reasons why a highly sensitive person should be a sought-after relationship in your life.

- They are able to manage conflicts well because they have the ability to observe and quickly diffuse a situation. Plus, they have a keen eye for details and can often sense a conflict erupting before it starts.
- They highly understand the needs of others and will work hard to keep their friends happy, including you.
- They like to involve others and help them grow. Even when you make a mistake, they will help you learn from it and maintain your confidence.
- They are not stuck in their own worlds.

- They have a sense of purpose and want to make a difference in people's lives.

If you are a highly sensitive person, know that you can be a great and valuable friend to many people out there.

Why Highly Sensitive People Make Great Employees

While highly sensitive people can struggle in major ways in many work environments, they actually make great employees. The attributes they have make them reliable, hardworking, intuitive, and great team players. Rarely will they cause drama. In fact, they will do their best to avoid it.

Highly sensitive people are often undervalued in the workplace. They are not the most charismatic or outspoken people in the office. In fact, they are probably the ones you will hear from the least. Unfortunately, the soft skills they bring to the table do not get the same recognition as the stronger skills. This does not mean they are less valuable as employees, though. The following are some of the reasons highly sensitive people are a great addition to any company.

- They are the ones you can count on. They have the right attitude, will always show up, and will put in the effort needed to get the job done.
- They are careful decision-makers and will rarely take action hastily. As a result, the decisions they make are often the best possible under the circumstances at the moment.

- If they are in a positive environment, they will thrive beyond your imagination.
- They can be creative and, therefore, find the right solutions to problems.
- People often think that leaders have to be loud and brash. Actually, this is the opposite of what a leader should be. True leaders are intuitive, listen well, and inspire others. This is why a highly sensitive person actually makes a great leader.
- Highly sensitive people will focus on what benefits the team, rather than what benefits themselves.

If you are a highly sensitive person, know that your attributes are truly desired in the workplace, even if it doesn't seem that way.

Guess what? As a highly sensitive person, you are special and bring a unique gift to this world. Too many people are stuck in their own heads and have no concept or understanding of the world around them. You, on the other hand, can acknowledge the thoughts and feelings of other people. Because of your great attributes, you must stop believing that you are undesirable or weak. You are actually the strong one. The next chapter will discuss how you can start believing in yourself and the value that you bring to the world. You will become a better person overall.

Chapter 3: Living As A Highly Sensitive Person

The key to living a happy life as a highly sensitive person is to embrace the good qualities that you possess and showcase them to the world, while not allowing your flaws to control you. The bad part about highly sensitive people is that their oversensitivity gets the best of them, and often at the most inopportune times. The goal of this chapter will be to focus on controlling your emotions and allowing your unique gifts to shine through by using specific action steps to rewire your brain and way of thinking. Mindset shifts will be a major factor in managing your habits and sensitivities. Once you go through the practices and action steps I discuss here; you will truly be able to live your best life as a highly sensitive person.

The first step in the process is realizing who you are. In the previous two chapters, I detailed the positive and negative attributes of a highly sensitive person. In the end, while having this trait has extreme downsides, the positives outweigh the negatives. If you have come to realize that you are a highly sensitive person, then it's time to move on to the strategies and actions steps to manage your emotions.

How To Overcome Your Sensitivities

Just to be clear, you will never get rid of your sensitivities. They have always been a part of who and always will be. The objective is to manage these sensitivities, so you can overcome them. If they control you, they can become a major obstacle. The key is to use them to your advantage by controlling them. The following are some survival tips for highly sensitive people so that they don't become overwhelmed.

- Get plenty of sleep. Usually, 7-8 hours is recommended, but whatever it takes t make you feel well-rested. A lack of sleep will make you irritable, moody, less productive, and decrease your concentration. Proper sleep will help soothe your senses.
- Eat healthy food throughout the day. People dismiss how much of an effect diet has on your mood. But, if you eat foods high in cholesterol, saturated fats, and sugars, you will become tired, irritable, and overly sensitive to stimuli.
- A good pair of headphones can keep you from getting triggered with loud noises. You cannot control the noise, but you can manage how much it affects you.
- Plan time to decompress. Being on the go all the time will always keep you on heightened alert. This means you will continuously be in a frazzled state of mind. Taking time to decompress, preferably at night, can allow your nerves to calm down and no longer be affected by external stimuli. Whatever you can do to isolate yourself from the craziness of the world, do it.
- Give yourself the time and space to get things done. Highly sensitive people do not do well with a packed schedule, so avoid getting yourself in this position if you can help it.
- Limit your caffeine intake. Caffeine is a natural stimulant that will make you feel jittery if taken in excess. Highly sensitive people might be even more sensitive to caffeine. If you drink two cups of coffee a day, cut it down to one.

- Try to avoid excessively lighted areas if you can. In your home, keep your lights dim, as well.
- Get your errands done during the off-hours. This means going out opposite the average person's regular schedule. Get your shopping done during the week, go out with friends on weeknights, and go to the gym early in the morning. The goal here is to avoid huge crowds that can stir up your emotions.
- Get out in nature as much as possible and get away from the hustle-and-bustle of the city.

Even though you are born being highly sensitive, there are still many environmental factors that can trigger you to become more over the top. The survival tips above are meant to prevent overloading your hypersensitive senses. Many psychologists and research scientists have stated that a proper lifestyle may not change our genetics, but it can keep it from making our issues worse.

Having Self-Esteem As A Highly Sensitive Person

Te thing that highly sensitive people struggle with the most is their self-esteem, which is the value and worth they place on themselves. This is because they allow their environment, including the people, around them, to dictate their emotions. It is difficult for these individuals to break away from the feeling other people are having. As a highly sensitive person yourself, it's time for you to start realizing the importance of self-esteem and begin to recognize ways you can improve your own. It is time to stop thinking you are not good enough. The following strategies will take a lot of practice, but once you start implementing them, you will notice major changes in your mindset.

Accept Thoughts, Emotions, And Sensations As They Are

All of these aspects are a part of you but do not define you. They are fleeting in nature and are changing from moment to moment. If you are feeling pain, whether emotional or physical, for a definitive moment, that does not mean you are weak. It is a sensation you are going through that will eventually pass. Instead of letting your thoughts and feeling control you, work on observing them objectively and then letting them go. Do not allow them to become attached to you.

Eliminate The Word "Should" From Your Vocabulary

When you use the word "should," it will elicit a sense of guilt inside of you. If you change it to "could," then you subconsciously open up your mind about what you could be doing and uses less judgment. Using the word "could" also showcases that there are many different options for us, and we are not required to stay on one path. Try it out:

"I should be going to the gym." Change it to, "I could be going to the gym." See the difference?

Do Not Rely On Other People For Self-Esteem

 Unfortunately, as highly sensitive people, most of our self-worth is dependent on what other people think of us. You will never place true value on yourself if this is the mindset you will carry. The major problem is that when our outside source for self-esteem vanishes, then the opinion we have of ourselves plummets. We have to internalize our power to create our value and become the sole person who is in charge of it.

Forgive

We all have something in our past that we are not proud of. We must learn to forgive ourselves for the mistakes we made so we can move on. We need to apply the same compassion for ourselves that we tend to show other people. The next time you are hard on yourself, imagine one of your best friends standing in your position. Now, picture what you would tell this person if they made the same mistakes you did. If it's something favorable, then tell yourself the same thing. Stop being your worst critic.

Take Stock Of Your Talents

We tend to focus on our faults, and this severely lowers our self-esteem. We do not give ourselves enough credit by doing this. It is time to take stock of your talents and remember the gifts that you bring to the world. Identify what you are good at. If you are having a tough time coming up with something, then start small. Perhaps you are good at putting things away. This is a good start. As you come up with things, write them down and keep them to look at constantly. Another exercise you can do is write down what you think you're not good at and then crumble up that piece of paper and throw it away. Focus on your positive attributes.

Remember that these exercises will take a lot of consistency. Do not just quit after one day. When you begin incorporating these strategies into your daily life, you will see vast improvements with your mindset.

Focusing On Jobs, You Are Good At

I discussed in the previous chapter about highly sensitive people being model employees. This is still true. However, the goal is to make yourself as happy as possible, and this means avoiding things that will trigger your sensitivities. That being said, there are certain environments and job types where a highly sensitive person will fit in better and even thrive. If you can avoid the stress altogether, then why not do so? The following are the best career options for you if you are a highly sensitive person.

Caring Professions

Careers that require a lot of caring and compassion will be right up a highly sensitive person's alley. These jobs include things like nursing, medicine, counseling, therapy, and coaching. These fields will target a highly sensitive person's strength. Bear in mind that certain areas, like the emergency department or the ICU, may be challenging areas for you. Also, any busy environment will have a lot of different emotions that you will have to contend with. Good options in these fields may be things like home health nursing or individual counseling.

Creative Endeavors

Highly sensitive people are often very creative, so they will thrive in professions where they can show off their creativity. Some of these roles include graphic designer, writer, photographer, artist, or architect. Many creative jobs can be done on a freelance basis, which allows you to create your own schedule. This will be a major benefit to you as a highly sensitive person.

Clergy

If you have a spiritual side to you, then working as a clergy person may be right for you. Bear in mind, that depending on the denomination, you may have to follow strict rules. This may cause difficulty if you are a highly open-minded person. Of course, if you can get over the structure, then your intuition and sensitivity will be valued and accepted.

Academia

With academia, you get to spend a significant amount of time doing thoughtful and intensive research on a subject you have an interest in. In addition, you get to teach your extensive knowledge to students; as a highly sensitive person, you will thrive in your areas. In the end, you are doing meaningful work throughout your profession.

IT Professional

Coding is a major portion of IT and requires a lot of creativity to be successful. You will also need strong intuition and an eye for detail. These are all qualities that are possessed by highly sensitive people. As one of these individuals, software engineering or website development might be the perfect career paths for you.

When choosing a career to go into, you should focus on your strengths and what areas you will be compatible with. Consider your strengths as a highly sensitive person and determine what line of work fits you best.

Dealing With Hyperarousal

There will be times when you are in a state of hyperarousal, where you will be wired up and out of control, physically and mentally. In some cases, hyperarousal can be a defense mechanism, like with the fight-or-flight response. In these moments, being on high alert is a necessity. However, when the hyperarousal goes beyond defined moments, you will be dealing with many problems, including stress, anxiety, and overall diminished emotional and physical health. Yes, being in a state of constant arousal is detrimental to your physical health. Prolonged stress has led to many chronic illnesses, like heart disease, stroke, diabetes, and even some cancers. In addition, mental health disorders like depression are also a possibility.

When you are in the hyperarousal state, you will have an increased heart rate, faster breathing, quicker reflexes, perspiration, and heightened sensitivity to stimuli. So, when you hear a loud noise, you will immediately jump into action, or at least be ready to. Once again, short-term physiological responses like these are not dangerous. If you are consistently in this state, then we have a problem that must be addressed.

Hyperarousal needs to be dealt with quickly; otherwise, it will take over your life. This response is a symptom of another problem, so if you can figure out that problem is, then you can address it directly. The following are some action steps that will have a favorable response to being wired.

Practice Mindfulness

The purpose of this technique is to sit peacefully and consciously observe the chaos and frantic thoughts going on inside your mind without trying to change them, escape from them, or fight them off. Many therapists use this technique with their clients because it is effective in getting over feelings of panic. It also helps to reduce your hyperarousal symptoms.

Perform this technique for about 1-5 minutes at a time. Just sit quietly and focus on your feelings of discomfort, agitation, and anxiety. Concentrate very hard in this area. See if you can visualize these negative feelings and imagine holding them in your arms. A common practice that therapists have their clients do is picture the problems they are holding as being much bigger and worse. It may sound confusing, but it works well for their clients. It is likely because once they've imagined the issue being worse, the thing does not seem as major.

Make Small Achievable Goals Towards Relaxation And Calmness

I do mean to make these goals achievable by keeping them small. When you first start out, shoot for 30 seconds of pure relaxations. Once you achieve this milestone, then try for one minute, then two minutes, and so on. Eventually, you will be able to be in this state for several minutes with no problems. Just work your way up.

It does not matter what relaxation techniques you use, as long as you are in a state of physical relaxation and calmness. This can mean lying down in bed, sitting in a comfortable chair, or meditating. The choice is yours. From here, remain quiet and focus on a body part that feels tense. Now, take one breath in slowly over a few seconds, then hold it for a few seconds before letting it out slowly. As you release the breath, imagine the tension leaving that part of the body you focused on earlier. Truly visualize the tension dissipating like a cloud of smoke.

Evaluate yourself after this. Did your breathing and pulse rate decrease? Do you feel less tense and anxious? If so, then the practice was a success. Keep working on this step to make yourself better.

Positive Self-Talk

In the middle of frantic self-talk that is negative, interrupt yourself and begin saying some encouraging phrases. These include statements like, "You will get through this," or "You are strong and will overcome." This technique will trick your mind and shift it from positive to negative. As a result, you will slow down your pace. Once you do this often, it will become a habit.

Investigate The Root Cause

The above exercises are beneficial; however, you should also determine what the root cause of your hyperarousal is. If you can figure this out, then the risk of flareups in the future will go down. Some of the causes include anxiety, PTSD, excess caffeine, and drug or alcohol use. Once you've narrowed it down, then you can focus on more specific techniques to eliminate the root cause.

For example, Cognitive Behavioral Therapy, or CBT, can be an effective strategy from anxiety. The goal of CBT is to challenge your current thought patterns through talk therapy. The following are a few key steps to make CBT work for you.

- Identify what you are thinking by actually writing them down on something. This way, you can visualize them.
- Assess your thoughts and realize that they may not be true or accurate. We often think negative thoughts for so long that we automatically assume they identify us, and we never challenge them.
- Replace these harmful thoughts with more positive and encouraging ones. Write down all of these new thoughts, as well.
- Now, read these new thoughts to yourself over and over again. Do this until it becomes a habit for you to think of these thoughts, which could take days or weeks.

CBT is a strategy that works for many different disorders, and therapists use it often.

The bottom line to all of this is that you will always be a highly sensitive person. It is not something you can avoid, nor should you try to do so. Despite the challenges that may exist, being a highly sensitive person is still a unique gift that you should embrace every day. Learning the techniques to control your thoughts and emotions, and not allowing your environment to overwhelm, you will ensure that you live a happy and satisfying life. Your sensitivity and intuitiveness are a true gift for many people.

www.ingramcontent.com/pod-product-compliance
Lightning Source LLC
Chambersburg PA
CBHW071621080526
44588CB00010B/1223